CHELSEA HOUSE PUBLISHERS
Modern Critical Views

Further titles in preparation.

Modern Critical Views

KATHERINE ANNE PORTER

Modern Critical Views

KATHERINE ANNE PORTER

Edited with an introduction by

Harold Bloom

Sterling Professor of the Humanities
Yale University

1986
CHELSEA HOUSE PUBLISHERS
New York
New Haven   Philadelphia

PROJECT EDITORS: Emily Bestler, James Uebbing
ASSOCIATE EDITOR: Maria Behan
EDITORIAL COORDINATOR: Karyn Gullen Browne
EDITORIAL STAFF: Laura Ludwig, Linda Grossman, Peter Childers
DESIGN: Susan Lusk

Cover illustration by Mark Sparacio

Library of Congress Cataloging in Publication Data

Katherine Anne Porter.
    (Modern critical views)
    Bibliography: p.
    Includes index.
    1. Porter, Katherine Anne, 1890–1980—Criticism and
interpretation—Addresses, essays, lectures.   I. Bloom,
Harold.   II. Series.
PS3531.0752Z69   1986   813'.52   85–17501
ISBN 0-87754-657-6

Chelsea House Publishers
Harold Steinberg, Chairman and Publisher
Susan Lusk, Vice President
A Division of Chelsea House Educational Communications, Inc.
133 Christopher Street, New York, NY 10014

Contents

Editor's Note

This volume brings together what in its editor's judgment constitutes the best criticism devoted to the fiction of Katherine Anne Porter. It begins with an "Introduction" that centers upon the story "Flowering Judas," in a reading that suggests we revise received critical judgments which have seen Laura, the story's heroine, as being somewhat culpable. Instead, the argument is made that Porter defines the narcissistic dilemma and even implicitly celebrates it, rather than judging and in any way disavowing it. I believe that the same aesthetic principle is at work in the stories concerning Miranda, Porter's own surrogate in her fiction.

The chronological sequence of this volume begins with Robert Penn Warren's superb essay, "Irony with a Center," which definitively establishes a critical context in which to perceive Porter's rhetorical stance. Two contrasting estimates of *Ship of Fools* follow, with Robert B. Heilman celebrating its stylistic affinities to Jane Austen and George Eliot, and Howard Moss praising its clarity but wondering at the novel's lack of "a hero and a heroic extravagance" and at its rather abstract treatment of love.

Eudora Welty's tribute to Porter emphasizes the spiritual and timeless element that is so movingly present in her own fiction as well. The deft reading of "Flowering Judas" by M. M. Liberman should juxtapose in suggestive agon with the analysis offered in my "Introduction." Where I see Laura's narcissistic investment of the self in her own ego, Liberman reads rather a self-betrayal, emptying out the ego and not constituting it.

A joint reading of the remarkable story "The Grave," by Constance Rooke and Bruce Wallis, makes a sound case for seeing it as a paradigm of the Fall. Joan Givner, Porter's biographer, usefully argues that the themes and concerns that eventually developed into *Ship of Fools* began during Porter's phase as a working journalist. With Thomas F. Walsh's account of "Pale Horse, Pale Rider," we are given an illuminating analysis of the marvelous short novel that centers upon Miranda's ambivalence towards love. This is followed by an absorbing application of Pascal's wager theory to Porter (and to Flannery O'Connor) by Joann P. Cobb.

Two opposed views of Porter's enigmatic story "He," by Bruce W. Jorgensen and Debra A. Moddelmog again demonstrate how Porter's work provokes antithetical readings. Where Jorgensen reads the story as authentic tragedy, Moddelmog insists upon a wholly ironic reading. Finally, Jane Krause DeMouy brings us a contemporary perspective from feminist criticism in her somber reading of "Old Mortality." One can prophesy that much of the future of Porter criticism will be involved with the continuing development of feminist literary studies.

Introduction

I

By the time she was fifty, Katherine Anne Porter had written and published nearly all the fiction for which she will be remembered. Her single novel, *Ship of Fools* (1962), seemed to me an interesting failure when I first read it, more than twenty years ago, and I now find it very difficult to read through for a second time. Its critical defenders have been numerous and distinguished, including Robert Penn Warren (certainly Porter's best critic), yet it is one of those books that calls out for defense. Perhaps its author waited too long to compose *Ship of Fools*, or perhaps her genius was so admirably suited to the short novel and the short story that it was condemned to languish at greater length. What seems clear is that Porter's lasting achievement is not in *Ship of Fools*, but in "Flowering Judas," "He," "Old Mortality," "Noon Wine," "Pale Horse, Pale Rider," "The Grave" and many of their companions. She is a supreme lyricist among story writers, molding her tales with the care and delicacy that Willa Cather (whom she greatly admired) gave to such novels as *My Ántonia* and *The Lost Lady*. Like Cather, she found her truest precursor in Henry James, though her formative work seems to me rather more indebted to Joyce's *Dubliners*. But, again like Cather, her sensibility is very different from that of her male precursors, and her art, original and vital, swerves away into a rhetorical stance and moral vision peculiarly her own.

I confess to loving "Flowering Judas" most among her works, though I recognize that the aesthetic achievement of "Old Mortality," "Noon Wine" and the stories grouped as "The Old Order," is a larger one. Still, "Flowering Judas" established Porter and rhetorically set a standard even she never surpassed. Its two most famous passages retain their aura:

> A brown, shock-haired youth came and stood in her patio one night and sang like a lost soul for two hours, but Laura could think of nothing to do about it. The moonlight spread a wash of gauzy silver over the clear spaces of the garden, and the shadows were cobalt blue. The scarlet blossoms of the Judas tree were dull purple, and the names of the colors

repeated themselves automatically in her mind, while she watched not the boy, but his shadow, fallen like a dark garment across the fountain rim, trailing in the water.

. . . No, said Laura, not unless you take my hand, no; and she clung first to the stair rail, and then to the topmost branch of the Judas tree that bent down slowly and set her upon the earth, and then to the rocky ledge of a cliff, and then to the jagged wave of a sea that was not water but a desert of crumbling stone. Where are you taking me, she asked in wonder but without fear. To death, and it is a long way off, and we must hurry, said Eugenio. No, said Laura, not unless you take my hand. Then eat these flowers, poor prisoner, said Eugenio in a voice of pity, take and eat: and from the Judas tree he stripped the warm bleeding flowers, and held them to her lips. She saw that his hand was fleshless, a cluster of small white petrified branches, and his eye sockets were without light, but she ate the flowers greedily for they satisfied both hunger and thirst. Murderer! said Eugenio, and Cannibal! This is my body and my blood. Laura cried No! and at the sound of her own voice, she awoke trembling, and was afraid to sleep again.

The allusiveness of these passages has been analyzed as being in the mode of T.S. Eliot; indeed the allusions generally are taken to involve Eliot's "Gerontion," where "Christ the tiger" came: "In depraved May, dogwood and chestnut, flowering judas, / To be eaten, to be divided, to be drunk / Among whispers." But Porter's story, intensely erotic, is neither a "Waste Land" allegory, nor a study of Christian nostalgia. Its beautiful, sleep-walking Laura is neither a betrayer nor a failed believer, but an aesthete, a storyteller poised upon the threshold of crossing over into her own art. Porter alternatively dated "Flowering Judas" in December 1929 or January 1930. She was not much aware of Freud, then or later, but he seemed to be aware of her, so to speak, in his extraordinary essay of 1914 on narcissism, which can be read, in some places, as a portrait of Porter's Laura, the beautiful enigma of "Flowering Judas":

. . . there arises in the woman a certain self-sufficiency (especially when there is a ripening into beauty) which compensates her for the social restrictions upon her object-choice. Strictly speaking, such women love only themselves with an intensity comparable to that of the man's love for them. Nor does their need lie in the direction of loving, but of being loved; and that man finds favour with them who fulfills this condition. The importance of this type of woman for the erotic life of mankind must be recognized as very great.

Freud goes on to observe that "one person's narcissism has a great attraction for those others who have renounced part of their own narcissism." Laura's curious coolness, which charms us into a sense of her inaccessibility, is the product not of her disillusion with either the Revolution or the Church, but of her childlike narcissism. Much of the lyrical strength of "Flowering Judas" comes from its superb contrast between the gray-eyed, grave Laura, who walks as beautifully as a dancer, and her obscene serenader, the professional revolutionist Braggioni, with his tawny yellow cat's eyes, his snarling voice, his gross intensity. Yet Braggioni is accurate when he tells Laura: "We are more alike than you realize in some things." Narcissist and self-loving leader of men share in a pragmatic cruelty, and in a vanity that negates the reality of all others:

> No matter what this stranger says to her, nor what her message to him, the very cells of her flesh reject knowledge and kinship in one monotonous word. No. No. No. She draws her strength from this one holy talismanic word which does not suffer her to be led into evil. Denying everything, she may walk anywhere in safety, she looks at everything without amazement.

It is Porter's art to place Laura beyond judgment. The dream-vision that ends the story is hardly a representation of a dream, since it is anything but a wish-fulfillment. It is the narcissist's ultimate reverie, an image of the Judas tree representing not betrayal so much as a revelation that the flowering Judas is oneself, one's perfect self-sufficiency. Laura, in the supposed dream or visionary projection, rightly transposes her status to that of Eugenio, the "poor prisoner," and greedily eats the Judas flowers "for they satisfied both hunger and thirst," as they must, being emblems of narcissistic self-passion, of the ego established by the self's investment in itself. When Eugenio cries out: "This is my body and my blood," he is mistaken, and we ought to give credence rather to Laura's outcry of "No!," which wakens her from her dream. It is again the same "one holy talismanic word which does not suffer her to be led into evil," the narcissist's rejection of any love-object except herself. It is Laura's body and Laura's blood that she never ceases to absorb, and it does satisfy her hunger and her thirst.

II

Porter is a superb instance of what Frank O'Connor called *The Lonely Voice*, his title for his book on the short story, where he begins by rejecting the traditional term for the genre:

> All I can say from reading Turgenev, Chekhov, Katherine Anne Porter, and others is that the very term "short story" is a misnomer. A great

story is not necessarily short at all, and the conception of the short story as a miniature art is inherently false. Basically, the difference between the short story and the novel is not one of length. It is a difference between pure and applied storytelling, and in case someone has still failed to get the point, I am not trying to decry applied storytelling. Pure storytelling is more artistic, that is all, and in storytelling I am not sure how much art is preferable to nature.

Porter too was not sure, and she deserves Robert Penn Warren's praise that hers "is a poetry that shows a deep attachment to the world's body." I add only that it shows also a deeper attachment to her own body, but I insist that is all to the good. Narcissism has gotten an absurdly bad name, but Freud certainly would snort at that, and so should we. A beautiful lyricist and a beautiful woman necessarily celebrate their own beauty, and Porter surpassingly was both. Even her stories' titles haunt me, just as photographs depicting her hold on in the memory. Warren rather surprisingly compares her to Faulkner, whose magnificence, unlike hers, generally does not come in particular phrases. I would prefer to compare her to Hart Crane, her difficult friend and impossible guest in Mexico, yet her truest contemporary, in the sense of a profound affinity in art. Porter's ambivalent account of Crane is at once a story by Porter and a visionary lyric of Hart Crane's:

> It was then that he broke into the monotonous obsessed dull obscenity which was the only language he knew after reaching a certain point of drunkenness, but this time he cursed things and elements as well as human beings. His voice at these times . . . stunned the ears and shocked the nerves and caused the heart to contract. In this voice and with words so foul there is no question of repeating them, he cursed separately and by name the moon, and its light: the heliotrope, the heaven-tree, the sweet-by-night, the star jessamine, and their perfumes. He cursed the air we breathed together, the pool of water with its two small ducks huddled at the edge, and the vines on the wall and house. But those were not the things he hated. He did not even hate us, for we were nothing to him. He hated and feared himself.

This is a great poet rushing towards self-destruction, his wounded narcissism converted into aggressivity against the self, which in turn fuels the death drive, beyond the pleasure principle. Implicit in Porter's memory of Crane is the trauma of betrayed affinity, as one great lyrical artist watches another take, not her downward path to wisdom, but the way down and out to death by water. Porter, a survivor, makes the paragraph into a frighteningly effective elegy for Crane, for that supreme lyricist whose gift has become a curse, to himself and to others. Like Crane,

Porter concentrated her gift, and her stories match his lyrics in their economy and in their sublime eloquence. Unlike him, she took care to survive, and perhaps we should praise her Laura, in "Flowering Judas," for the wisdom to survive, rather than condemn her for not offering herself up to be devoured by a violent though beautiful reality.

ROBERT PENN WARREN

Irony with a Center

The fiction of Katherine Anne Porter, despite widespread critical adulation, has never found the public which its distinction merits. Many of her stories are unsurpassed in modern fiction, and some are not often equaled. She belongs to the relatively small group of writers—extraordinarily small, when one considers the vast number of stories published every year in English and American magazines—who have done serious, consistent, original, and vital work in the form of short fiction—the group which would include James Joyce, Katherine Mansfield, Sherwood Anderson, and Ernest Hemingway. This list does not include a considerable number of other writers who, though often finding other forms more congenial—the novel or poetry—have scored occasional triumphs in the field of short fiction. Then, of course, there is a very large group of writers who have a great facility, a great mechanical competence, and sometimes moments of real perception, but who work from no fundamental and central conviction.

It was once fashionable to argue complacently that the popular magazine had created the short story—had provided the market and had cultivated an appetite for the product. It is true that the magazine did provide the market, but at the same time, and progressively, the magazine has corrupted the short story. What the magazine encourages is not so much the short story as a conscious or unconscious division of the artistic self of the writer. One can still discover (as in an address delivered by Mr. Frederick Lewis Allen to the American Philosophical Society) a genial self-congratulation in the face of "mass appreciation." But, writes Mr. R. P. Blackmur in reply:

From *Selected Essays of Robert Penn Warren.* Copyright © 1941 and 1969 by Robert Penn Warren. Random House, Inc.

In fact, mass appreciation of the kind which Mr. Allen approves represents the constant danger to the artist of any serious sort: *the danger of popularization before creation.* . . . The difference between great art and popular art is relatively small; but the difference between either and popularized art is radical, and absolute. Popular art is topical and natural, great art is deliberate and thematic. What can be popularized in either is only what can be sold . . . a scheme which requires the constant replacement of the shoddy goods. He (Mr. Allen) does not mean to avow this; he no doubt means the contrary; but there it is. Until American or any other society is educated either up to the level or back to the level of art with standards, whether popular or great, it can be sold nothing but art without standards. . . .

The fact that Miss Porter has not attempted a compromise may account for the relatively small body of her published fiction. There was the collection of stories published in 1931 under the title *Flowering Judas*; an enlarged collection, under the same title in 1935, which includes two novelettes, "The Cracked Looking-Glass" and "Hacienda," the latter of which had been previously published by Harrison, in Paris; a collection of three novelettes under the title *Pale Horse, Pale Rider*, in 1939; the Modern Library edition of *Flowering Judas*; and a few pieces, not yet in book form, which have appeared in various magazines—for instance, sections of the uncompleted biography of Cotton Mather and the brilliant story "A Day's Work." (Since included in the volume *The Leaning Tower*).

Her method of composition does not, in itself, bend readily to the compromise. In many instances, a story or novelette has not been composed straight off. Instead, a section here and a section there have been written— little germinal scenes explored and developed. Or scenes or sketches of character which were never intended to be incorporated in the finished work have been developed in the process of trying to understand the full potentiality of the material. One might guess at an approach something like this: a special, local excitement provoked by the material—character or incident; an attempt to define the nature of that local excitement, as local—to squeeze it and not lose a drop; an attempt to understand the relationships of the local excitements and to define the implications— to arrive at theme; the struggle to reduce theme to pattern. That would seem to be the natural history of the characteristic story. Certainly, it is a method which requires time, scrupulosity, and contemplation.

The method itself is an index to the characteristics of Miss Porter's fiction—the rich surface detail scattered with apparently casual profuseness and the close structure which makes such detail meaningful; the great compression and economy which one discovers upon analysis; the precision of psychology and observation, the texture of the style.

Most reviewers, commenting upon Miss Porter's distinction, refer to her "style"—struck, no doubt, by an exceptional felicity of phrase, a precision in the use of metaphor, and a subtlety of rhythm. It is not only the appreciation of the obviously poetical strain in Miss Porter's work that has tended to give her reputation some flavor of the special and exquisite, but also the appreciation of the exceptional precision of her language. When one eminent critic praises her for an "English of a purity and precision almost unique in contemporary American fiction," he is giving praise richly merited and praise for a most important quality, but this praise, sad to relate as a commentary on our times, is a kind that does encourage the special reputation. This same eminent critic also praises Miss Porter as an artist, which goes to say that he himself knows very well that her language is but one aspect of her creations; but even so, the word *artist* carries its own overtones of exquisiteness.

The heart of the potential reader may have been chilled—and I believe quite rightly—by the praise of "beautiful style." He is put off by a reviewer's easy abstracting of style for comment and praise; his innocence repudiates the fallacy of agreeable style. The famous common reader is not much concerned with English as such, pure or impure, precise or imprecise, and he is no more concerned with the artist as artist. He is concerned with what the English will say to him, and with what the artist will do for him, or to him.

It is, of course, just and proper for us to praise Miss Porter for her English and her artistry, but we should remind ourselves that we prize those things because she uses them to create vivid and significant images of life. All this is not to say that we are taking the easy moralistic, or easy Philistine, view of English or artistry. We know that the vividness and the significance of any literary work exist only in the proper medium, and that only because of a feeling for the medium and an understanding of artistry did the writer succeed, in the first place, in discovering vividness and significance. We hope that we shall never have to remind ourselves of that fact, and now we remind ourselves of the vividness and significance in which Miss Porter's English and artistry eventuate, only because we would balance praise for the special with praise for the general, praise for subtlety with praise for strength, praise for sensibility with praise for intellect.

But let us linger upon the matter of Miss Porter's style in the hope that it can be used as a point of departure. Take, for example, a paragraph from the title story of *Flowering Judas*, the description of Braggioni, the half-Italian, half-Indian revolutionist in Mexico, "a leader of men, skilled revolutionist, and his skin has been punctured in honorable warfare." His followers "warm themselves in his reflected glory and say to each other,

'He has a real nobility, a love of humanity raised above mere personal affections.' The excess of this self-love has flowed out, inconveniently for her, over Laura"—the puzzled American girl who has been lured to Mexico by revolutionary enthusiasm and before whom he sits with his guitar and sings sentimental songs, while his wife weeps at home. But here is the passage:

> Braggioni . . . leans forward, balancing his paunch between his spread knees, and sings with tremendous emphasis, weighing his words. He has, the song relates, no father and no mother, nor even a friend to console him; lonely as a wave of the sea he comes and goes, lonely as a wave. His mouth opens round and yearns sideways, his balloon cheeks grow oily with the labor of song. He bulges marvelously in his expensive garments. Over his lavender collar, crushed upon a purple necktie, held by a diamond hoop: over his ammunition belt of tooled leather worked in silver, buckled cruelly around his gasping middle: over the tops of his glossy yellow shoes Braggioni swells with ominous ripeness, his mauve silk hose stretched taut, his ankles bound with the stout leather thongs of his shoes.
>
> When he stretches his eyelids at Laura she notes again that his eyes are the true tawny yellow cat's eyes. He is rich, not in money, he tells her, but in power, and this power brings with it the blameless ownership of things, and the right to indulge his love of small luxuries. "I have a taste for the elegant refinements," he said once, flourishing a yellow silk handkerchief before her nose. "Smell that? It is Jockey Club, imported from New York." Nonetheless, he is wounded by life. He will say so presently. "It is true everything turns to dust in the hand, to gall on the tongue." He sighs and his leather belt creaks like a saddle girth.

The passage is sharp and evocative. Its phrasing embodies a mixture, a fusion, of the shock of surprise and the satisfaction of precision—a resolved tension, which may do much to account for the resonance and vibration of the passage. We have in it the statement, "His mouth opens round and yearns sideways"—and we note the two words *yearns* and *sideways*; in the phrase, "labor of song"; in, "he bulges marvelously"; in, "Braggioni swells with ominous ripeness." But upon inspection it may be discovered that the effect of these details is not merely a local effect. The subtle local evocations really involve us in the center of the scene; we are taken to the core of the meaning of the scene, and thence to the central impulse of the story; and thence, possibly to the germinal idea of all of this author's fiction. All of these filaments cannot be pursued back through the web—the occasion does not permit; but perhaps a few can be traced to the meaning of the scene itself in the story.

What we have here is the revolutionist who loves luxury, who feels that power gives blameless justification to the love of elegant refinements, but whose skin has been punctured in "honorable warfare"; who is a competent leader of men, but who is vain and indolent; who is sentimental and self-pitying, but, at the same time, ruthless; who betrays his wife and yet, upon his return home, will weep with his wife as she washes his feet and weeps; who labors for the good of man, but is filled with self-love.

We have here a tissue of contradictions, and the very phraseology takes us to these contradictions. For instance, the word *yearns* involves the sentimental, blurred emotion, but immediately afterward the words *sideways* and *oily* remind us of the grossness, the brutality, the physical appetite. So then the implied paradox in the "labor of song." The ammunition belt, we recall, is buckled *cruelly* about his "gasping middle." The ammunition belt reminds us that this indolent, fat, apparently soft, vain man is capable of violent action, is a man of violent profession, and sets the stage for the word *cruelly*, which involves the paradox of the man who loves mankind and is capable of individual cruelties, and which, further, reminds us that he punishes himself out of physical vanity and punishes himself by defining himself in his calling—the only thing that belts in his sprawling, meaningless animality. He swells with "ominous ripeness"—and we sense the violent threat in the man as contrasted with his softness, a kind of great overripe plum as dangerous as a grenade, a feeling of corruption mixed with sentimental sweetness; and specifically we are reminded of the threat to Laura in the situation. We come to the phrase "wounded by life," and we pick up again the motif hinted at in the song and in the lingering rhythms: "He has, the song relates, no father and no mother, nor even a friend to console him; lonely as a wave of the sea he comes and goes, lonely as a wave." In nothing is there to be found a balm—not in revolution, in vanity, in love—for the "vast cureless wound of his self-esteem." Then, after the bit about the wound, we find the sentence: "He sighs and his leather belt creaks like a saddle girth." The defeated, sentimental sigh, the cureless wound, and the bestial creaking of the leather.

If this reading of the passage is acceptable, the passage itself is a rendering of the problem which the character of Braggioni poses to Laura. It is stated, in bare, synoptic form, elsewhere:

> The gluttonous bulk of Braggioni has become a symbol of her many disillusions, for a revolutionist should be lean, animated by heroic faith, a vessel of abstract virtues. This is nonsense, she knows it now and is ashamed of it. Revolution must have leaders, and leadership is a career for energetic men. She is, her comrades tell her, full of romantic error, for what she defines as a cynicism is to them merely a developed sense of reality.

What is the moral reality here? This question is, I should say, the theme of the story, which exists in an intricate tissue of paradox, and is posed only in the dream Laura has at the end, a dream which embodies but does not resolve the question.

With all the enchanting glitter of style and all the purity of language and all the flow and flicker of feeling, Miss Porter's imagination, as a matter of fact, is best appreciated if we appreciate its essential austerity, its devotion to the fact drenched in God's direct daylight, its concern with the inwardness of character, and its delight in the rigorous and discriminating deployment of a theme. Let us take another passage from her work, a passage from the novelette "Noon Wine," the description of Mr. Thompson, a poor dirt-farmer in Texas, busy at his churning, a task that he, in his masculine pride and bitter incompetence, finds contemptible and demeaning:

> Mr. Thompson was a tough weather-beaten man with stiff black hair and a week's growth of black whiskers. He was a noisy proud man who held his neck so straight his whole face stood level with his Adam's apple, and the whiskers continued down his neck and disappeared into a black thatch under his open collar. The churn rumbled and swished like the belly of a trotting horse, and Mr. Thompson seemed somehow to be driving a horse with one hand, reining it in and urging it forward; and every now and then he turned halfway around and squirted a tremendous spit of tobacco juice out over the steps. The door stones were brown and gleaming with fresh tobacco juice.

This passage is simple and unpretending, a casual introductory description near the beginning of a story, but it succeeds in having its own kind of glitter and purity and flow. Here those things come, as in so much of Miss Porter's fiction, from the writer's rigorous repudiation of obvious literary resources, resources which, on other occasions, she can use so brilliantly. The things that stir our admiration in the passage from "Flowering Judas" are notably absent here, are notably eschewed. Here the style is of the utmost transparency, and our eye and ear are captivated by the very ordinariness of the ordinary items presented to us, the trotting motion of the churn, the swish of the milk, the tobacco juice glittering on the door stones. Miss Porter has the power of isolating common things, the power that Chekhov or Frost or Ibsen or, sometimes, Pound has, the power to make the common thing glow with an Eden-innocence by the mere fact of the isolation. It is a kind of indicative poetry.

Miss Porter's eye and ear, however, do not seize with merely random and innocent delight on the objects of the world, even though we may take that kind of delight in the objects she so lovingly places before us, transmuted in their ordinariness. If the fact drenched in daylight commands her unfaltering devotion, it is because such facts are in themselves a deep language, or can be made to utter a language of the deepest burden. What are the simple facts saying in the paragraph just quoted?

They are saying something about Mr. Thompson, poor Mr. Thompson who will die of a self-inflicted gunshot wound before many pages have passed, and will die of it because he is all the things we might have surmised of him if we had been able to understand beforehand the language of the simple facts of the scene at the churn. The pridefully stiff neck and the black whiskers, they tell us something. He is the sort of man who ought, or thinks he ought, to be holding the reins of a spanking horse and not the cord of a churn, and his very gesture has a kind of childish play acting. Somewhere in his deepest being, he is reminded of the spanking horse with the belly swishing in the trot, the horse such a fine manly man ought to have under his hand, if luck just weren't so ornery and unreasonable, and so he plays the game with himself. But he can't quite convince himself. It is only a poor old churn, after all, woman's work on a rundown and debt-bit shirt-tail farm, with kids and an ailing wife, and so he spits his tremendous spits of masculine protest against fate, and the brown juice gleams with its silly, innocent assertiveness on the stones the woman's broom has, so many times, swept clean of this and that. In the end, looking back, we can see that the story is the story of a noisy, proud, stiff-necked man whose pride has constantly suffered under failure, who salves his hurt pride by harmless bluster with his wife and children, and who, in the end, stumbles into a situation which takes the last prop of certainty from his life.

Our first glimpse of Mrs. Thompson is in the "front room," where she lies with the green shade down and a wet cloth over her poor weak eyes. But in spite of the weeping eyes, the longing for the cool dark, and all her sad incompetence, on the one hand, and Mr. Thompson's bluster and hurt pride on the other, there is a warm secret life between them:

> "Tell *you* the truth, Ellie," said Mr. Thompson, picking his teeth with a fork and leaning back in the best of humors, "I always thought your granma was a ter'ble ole fool. She'd just say the first thing that popped into her head and call it God's wisdom."
>
> "My granma wasn't anybody's fool. Nine times out of ten she knew what she was talking about. I always say, the first thing you think is the best thing you can say."
>
> "Well," said Mr. Thompson, going into another shout, "you're so reefined about that goat story, you just try speaking out in mixed comp'ny sometime! You just try it. S'pose you happened to be thinking about a hen and a rooster, hey? I reckon you'd shock the Babtist preacher!" He

gave her a good pinch on her thin little rump. "No more meat on you than a rabbit," he said, fondly. "Now I like 'em cornfed."

Mrs. Thompson looked at him open-eyed and blushed. She could see better by lamplight. "Why, Mr. Thompson, sometimes I think you're the evilest-minded man that ever lived." She took a handful of hair on the crown of his head and gave it a good, slow pull. "That's to show you how it feels, pinching so hard when you're supposed to be playing," she said, gently.

This little glimpse of their secret life, Mr. Thompson's masculine, affectionate bragging and bullying and teasing, and Mrs. Thompson's shy and embarrassed playfulness, comes as a surprise in the middle of their drab world, a sudden brightness and warmth. Without this episode we should never get the full force of Mr. Thompson's bafflement and anger when Mr. Hatch, the baleful stranger, misinterprets Mr. Thompson's prideful talk of his wife's ill health and says that he himself would get rid of a puny wife mighty quick. And without this episode we should never sense how that bafflement and anger flow, as one more component, into the moment when Mr. Thompson sees, or thinks he sees, the blade of Mr. Hatch's bowie knife go into the poor Swede's stomach, and he brings his axe down on Hatch's head, as though stunning a beef.

We are, however, getting ahead of ourselves. Let us summarize the apparently simple story. On Mr. Thompson's poverty-bit farm a stranger appears, a Swede, Mr. Helton, who takes work at a low wage, plays the harmonica in his off hours, and seems to inhabit some vague and lonely inner world. But Mr. Helton is a worker, and for the first time the farm begins to pay. Mr. Thompson can give up "woman's work," can do the big important things that become a man, and can bask in the new prosperity. Nine years later, to interrupt the new prosperity, another stranger appears, a Mr. Hatch, who reveals that the Swede is a murderer and a lunatic whom he will arrest and take back north to the asylum. When the Swede appears, Mr. Thompson sees, or thinks he sees, Mr. Hatch's knife going into his stomach. With his axe he kills Mr. Hatch, defending the Swede, defending what, he does not know.

After the deed, there isn't, strangely enough, a scratch on the Swede's stomach. This doesn't bother the jury, and Mr. Thompson is acquitted in no time at all. But it does bother Mr. Thompson. He simply can't understand things, how he could see the knife go in and then find it not true, and all the other things he can't understand. He had never intended to do it, he was just protecting the poor Swede. But we are aware that there had been the slow building up of the mysterious anger against Mr. Hatch, of the fear that Mr. Hatch threatened the new prosperity of the farm. And in the trial Mr. Thompson has been caught in a web of little lies, small distortions of fact, nothing serious, nothing needed to prove he wasn't guilty, just little twists to make everything clearer and simpler.

Is Mr. Thompson innocent or guilty? He doesn't really know. Caught in the mysteriousness of himself, caught in all the impulses which he had never been able to face, caught in all the little lies which had really meant no harm, he can't know the truth about anything. He can't stand the moral uncertainty of this situation, but he does not know what it is that most deeply he can't stand. He can't stand not knowing what he himself really is. His pride can't stand that kind of nothingness. Not knowing what it is he can't stand, he is under the compulsion to go, day after day, around the countryside, explaining himself, explaining how he had not meant to do it, how it was defense of the Swede, how it was self-defense, all the while plunging deeper and deeper into the morass of his fate. Then he finds that his own family have, all along, thought him guilty. So the proud man has to kill himself to prove, in his last pride, that he is really innocent.

That, however, is the one thing that can never be proved, for the story is about the difficult definition of guilt and innocence. Mr. Thompson, not able to trust his own innocence, or understand the nature of whatever guilt is his, has taken refuge in the lie, and the lie, in the end, kills him. The issue here, as in "Flowering Judas," is not to be decided simply. It is, in a sense, left suspended, the terms defined, but the argument left only at a provisional resolution. Poor Mr. Thompson— innocent and yet guilty, and in his pride unable to live by the provisional.

"The Cracked Looking-Glass," too, is about guilt and innocence. It is the story of a high-spirited, pleasure-loving Irish girl, married to a much older man, faithful to him, yet needing the society of young fun-provoking men, to whom she takes a motherly or sisterly attitude. She lives a kind of lie—in fact, she can't tell anything without giving it a romantic embroidery. Then she is horrified to discover that her Connecticut neighbors think her a bad woman, suspect her of infidelities. At the end, sitting in her tight kitchen with Old Dennis, "while beyond were far off places full of life and gaiety . . . and beyond everything like a green field with morning sun on it lay youth and Ireland," she leans over and puts her hand on her husband's knee, and asks him, in an ordinary voice: "Whyever did ye marry a woman like Me?"

Dennis says mind, she doesn't tip the chair over, and adds that he knew he could never do better. Then:

She sat up and felt his sleeves carefully. "I want you to wrap up warm this bitter weather, Dennis," she told him. "With two pairs of socks and the chest protector, for if anything happened to you, whatever would become of me in this world?"

"Let's not think of it," said Dennis, shuffling his feet.

"Let's not, then," said Rosaleen. "For I could cry if you crooked a finger at me."

Again the provisional resolution of the forces of the story: not a solution which Rosaleen can live by with surety, but one which she must re-learn and re-earn every day.

With the theme of "The Cracked Looking-Glass" in mind, let us take another of the novelettes, "Old Mortality."

To begin, "Old Mortality" is relatively short, some twenty thousand words, but it gives an impression of the mass of a novel. One factor contributing to this effect is the length of the time span; the novelette falls into three sections, dated 1885–1902, 1904, and 1912. Another factor is the considerable number of the characters, who, despite the brevity of the story, are sketched in with great precision; we know little about them, but that little means much. Another, and not quite so obvious but perhaps more important, factor is the rich circumstantiality and easy discursiveness, especially in Part I, which sets the tone of the piece. The author lingers on anecdote, apparently just to relish the anecdote, to extract the humor or pathos—but in the end we discover that there has been no casual self-indulgence, or indulgence of the reader; the details of the easy anecdote, which seemed to exist at the moment for itself alone, have been working busily in the cellarage of our minds.

Part I, 1885–1902, introduces us to two little girls, Maria and Miranda, aged twelve and eight, through whose eyes we see the family. There is the grandmother, who takes no part in the action of the story, but whose brief characterization, we discover, is important—the old lady who, "twice a year compelled in her blood by the change of seasons, would sit nearly all day beside old trunks and boxes in the lumber room, unfolding layers of garments and small keepsakes . . . unwrapping locks of hair and dried flowers, crying gently and easily as if tears were the only pleasure she had left." (Her piety—stirred by the equinoxes, as unreflecting as tropism—provides the basic contrast for the end of the story; her piety does not achieve the form of legend—merely a compulsion of the blood, the focus of old affections.) There is the father, "a pleasant everyday sort of man"—who once shot to protect the family "honor" and had to run to Mexico. There is Cousin Eva, chinless and unbeautiful amidst the belles, who, when we first meet her, teaches Latin in a female seminary and tries to interest Maria and Miranda in that study by telling them the story of John Wilkes Booth, "who, handsomely garbed in a long black cloak"—so the story is recast by the little girls—"had leaped to the stage after assassinating President Lincoln. 'Sic semper tyrannis,' he had shouted superbly, in spite of his broken leg." There is Amy, dead, already a legend, a beautiful sad family story, the girl who almost had a duel fought over her in New Orleans, who drove her suitor, Cousin Gabriel, almost to distraction before she married him, and who died under mysterious circumstances a few weeks after her marriage. There is Gabriel himself, fond of the races, cut off by his grandfather without a penny, a victim of the bottle in his bereavement; he marries Miss Honey, who can never compete with the legend of the dead Amy. In this section, the little girls attempt to make the people they know and the stories they have heard fit together, make sense; and always at the center is the story of Amy.

Part II, in contrast with Part I with its discursiveness, its blurring of time, its anecdotal richness, gives a single fully developed scene, dated 1904. The father takes the little girls, on holiday from their convent school, to the races. There, out of family piety, they bet their dollar on Uncle Gabriel's horse—a poor hundred-to-one shot. (Piety and common sense—they know even at their tender years that a hundred-to-one bet is no bet at all—are in conflict, and piety wins only because of the father's pressure.) But Gabriel's horse comes in, and they see for the first time their romantic Uncle Gabriel—"a shabby fat man with bloodshot blue eyes . . . and a big melancholy laugh like a groan"—now drunk, and after his victory, weeping. But he takes them to meet Miss Honey, Amy's successor, in his shabby apartment, and the little girls know that Miss Honey hates them all.

Part III, 1912, shows us Miranda on a train going to the funeral of Uncle Gabriel, who has died in Lexington, Kentucky, but has been brought home to lie beside Amy—to whom he belongs. On the train Miranda, now a young lady recently married, meets Cousin Eva, whom she has not seen for many years, who has, since the days at the seminary, crusaded for woman suffrage and gone to jail for her convictions. The talk goes back to the family story, to Amy. "Everybody loved Amy," Miranda remarks, but Cousin Eva replies: "Not everybody by a long shot. . . . She had enemies. If she knew she pretended she didn't. . . . She was sweet as honeycomb to everybody. . . . That was the trouble. She went through life like a spoiled darling, doing as she pleased and letting other people suffer for it." Then: " 'I never believed for one moment,' says Cousin Eva, putting her mouth close to Miranda's ear and breathing peppermint hotly into it, 'that Amy was an impure woman. Never! But let me tell you there were plenty who did believe it.' " So Cousin Eva begins to reinterpret the past, all the romantic past, the legend of Amy, who, according to Cousin Eva, was not beautiful, just good-looking, whose illness hadn't been romantic, and who had, she says, committed suicide.

Cousin Eva defines the bitter rivalry under the gaiety of the legend, the vicious competition among the belles. And more:

> Cousin Eva wrung her hands. "It was just sex," she said in despair; [The word *despair*, caught in the frustrated and yet victorious old woman's casual gesture, is important—a resonance from her personal story which gives an echo to the theme of the story itself.] "their minds dwelt on nothing else. They didn't call it that, it was all smothered under pretty names, but that's all it was, sex."

So Cousin Eva, who has given her life to learning and a progressive cause, defines all the legend in terms of economics and biology. "They simply festered inside," she says of all the Amys, "they festered."

But Miranda, catching a Baudelairean vision of "corruption concealed under lace and flowers," thinks quite coldly: "Of course, it was not like that. This is no more true than what I was told before, it's every bit as romantic." And in revulsion from Cousin Eva, she wants to get home, though she is grown and married now, and see her father and sister, who are solid and alive, are not merely "definitions."

But when she arrives her father cannot take her in, in the old way. He turns to Cousin Eva. And the two old people, who represent the competing views of the past—love and poetry opposed to biology and economics—sit down together in a world, their world of the past, which excludes Miranda, Miranda thinks: "Where are my own people and my own time?" She thinks, and the thought concludes the story: "Let them go on explaining how things happened. I don't care. At least I can know the truth about what happens to me, she assured herself silently, making a promise to herself, in her hopefulness, her ignorance."

So much for the action of the story. We see immediately that it is a story about legend, and it is an easy extension to the symbol for tradition, the meaning of the past for the present. We gradually become acquainted with the particular legend through the little girls, but the little girls themselves, in their innocence, criticize the legend. Their father, speaking of Amy's slimness, for instance, says: "There were never any fat women in the family, thank God." But the little girls remember Aunt Keziah, in Kentucky, who was famous for her heft. (Such an anecdote is developed richly and humorously, with no obvious pointing to the theme, beyond the logic of the context.) Such details, in Part I, develop the first criticism of the legend, the criticism by innocent common sense. In Part II, the contrast between Gabriel as legend and Gabriel as real extends the same type of criticism, but more dramatically; but here another, a moral criticism, enters in, for we have the effect of Amy on other people's lives, on Gabriel and Miss Honey. This, however, is not specified; it merely charges the scene of the meeting between Miranda and Cousin Eva on the way to Gabriel's funeral. Part III at first gives us, in Cousin Eva's words, the modern critical method applied to the legend—as if invoking Marx and Freud.

Up to this point, the line of the story has been developed fairly directly, though under a complicated surface. The story could end here, a story of repudiation, and some readers have interpreted it as such. But—and here comes the first reversal of the field—Miranda repudiates Cousin Eva's version, as romantic, too, in favor of the "reality" of her father, whom she is soon to see. But there is another shift. Miranda discovers that she is cut off from her father, who turns to Cousin Eva, whose "myth" contradicts his "myth," but whose world he can share. Miranda, cut off, determines to leave them to their own sterile pursuit of trying to understand the past. She will understand herself, the truth of what happens to her. This would provide another point of rest for the story—a story about the brave younger generation, their hope, courage, and honesty, and some readers have taken it thus. But—withheld cunningly until the end, until the last few words—there is a last reversal of the field. Miranda makes her promise to herself in "her hopefulness, her ignorance." And those two words, *hopefulness, ignorance*, suddenly echo throughout the story.

Miranda will find *a* truth, as it were, but it, too, will be a myth, for it will not be translatable, or, finally, communicable. But it will be the only truth she can win, and for better or worse she will have to live by it. She must live by her own myth. But she must earn her myth in the process of living. Her myth will be a new myth, different from the mutually competing myths of her father and Cousin Eva, but stemming from that antinomy. Those competing myths will simply provide the terms of her own dialectic of living.

We remember that the heroine's name is Miranda, and we may remember Miranda of Shakespeare's *Tempest*, who exclaims, "O brave new world, that has such people in it!" Perhaps the identity of the name is not an accident. Miranda of "Old Mortality" has passed a step beyond that moment of that exclamation, but she, too, has seen the pageant raised by Prospero's wand—the pageant evoked by her father, the pleasant everyday sort of father, who, however, is a Prospero, though lacking the other Prospero's irony. For "Old Mortality," like *The Tempest*, is about illusion and reality, and comes to rest upon a perilous irony.

In "Old Mortality" Miss Porter has used very conventional materials; the conventional materials, however, are revitalized by the intellectual scope of the interpretation and the precision and subtlety of structure. But Miss Porter has not committed herself to one type of material. The world of balls and horsemanship and romance is exchanged in "Noon Wine," as we have seen, for a poverty-ridden Texas farm; in "Pale Horse, Pale Rider," for a newspaper office and a rooming house at the time of World War I; in "Hacienda," "Flowering Judas," and "María Concepción," for Mexico. We may ask, What is the common denominator of these stories, aside from the obvious similarities of style (though the style itself is very flexible)? What is the central "view," the central intuition?

In these stories, and, as I believe, in many others, there is the same paradoxical problem of definition, the same delicate balancing of rival considerations, the same scrupulous development of competing claims to attention and action, the same interplay of the humorous and the serious, the same refusal to take the straight line, the formula, through the material at hand. This has implied for some readers that the underlying attitude is one of skepticism, negation, refusal to confront the need for immediate, watertight, foolproof solutions. The skeptical and ironical bias is, I think, important in Miss Porter's work, and it is true that her work wears an air of detachment and contemplation. But, I should say, her irony is an irony with a center, never an irony for irony's sake. It simply implies, I think, a refusal to accept the formula, the ready-made solution, the hand-me-down morality, the word for the spirit. It affirms, rather, the constant need for exercising discrimination, the arduous obligation of the intellect in the face of conflicting dogmas, the need for a dialectical approach to matters of definition, the need for exercising as much of the human faculty as possible.

This basic attitude finds its correlation in her work, in the delicacy of phrase, the close structure, the counterpoint of incident and implication. That is, a story must test its thematic line at every point against its total circumstantiality; the thematic considerations must, as it were, be validated in terms of circumstance and experience, and never be resolved in the poverty of statement.

In one sense, it is the intellectual rigor and discrimination that gives Miss Porter's work its classic distinction and control—that is, if any one quality can be said to be uniquely responsible. No, no single quality can take that credit, but where many writers have achieved stories of perception, feeling, sensibility, strength, or charm, few have been able to achieve stories of a deep philosophic urgency in the narrow space, and fewer still have been able to achieve the kind of thematic integration of a body of stories, the mark of the masters, the thing that makes us think first of the central significance of a writer rather than of some incidental and individual triumph. For Miss Porter's bright indicative poetry is, at long last, a literally metaphysical poetry, too. The luminosity is from inward.

ROBERT B. HEILMAN

"Ship of Fools":
Notes on Style

Katherine Anne Porter is sometimes
thought of as a stylist. "Stylist" is likely to call up unclear images of
coloratura, acrobatics, elaborateness of gesture, a mingling of formalism
probably euphuistic with conspicuous private variations, like fingerprints.
It might call to mind Edward Dahlberg's peremptory dense texture of
crusty archaism and thorny image, a laboriously constructed thicket so
well guarding the estate of his mind that it often becomes that estate. It is
not so with Miss Porter. There is nothing of arresting facade in her style,
nothing of showmanship. Though on the lecture platform she can be all
showman, and slip into the prima donna, in her proper medium both the
public personality and the private being vanish from the stage. At least
they are not easily detectable presences. In *Ship of Fools* the style is a
window of things and people, not a symbolic aggression of ego upon them.
It seems compelled by the objects in the fiction; it is their visible surface,
the necessary verbal form that makes their identity perceivable. It seems
never the construction of an artist imposing, from her own nature, an
arbitrary identity upon inert materials, but rather an emanation of the
materials themselves, finding through the artist as uninterfering medium
the stylistic mold proper to their own nature. Miss Porter is ruling all, of
course, but she seems not to be ruling at all: hence of her style we use
such terms as "distance," "elegance," and of course the very word for what
she seems to have ceded, "control." She is an absentee presence: in one

From *Katherine Anne Porter: A Critical Symposium,* edited by George Core and Lodwick
Hartley. Copyright © 1969 by University of Georgia Press.

sense her style is no-style. No-style is what it will seem if style means some notable habit of rhythm or vocabulary, some uninterchangeable (though not unborrowable) advice that firmly announces "Faulkner" or "Hemingway." Miss Porter has no "signal" or call letters that identify a single station of wave length. She does not introduce herself or present herself. Much less does she gesticulate. She does not pray on street corners; wrestle with her subject in public as if she were barely managing to throw a troublesome devil; or lash her tail and arch her back like a cat demonstrating expertise with a mouse. She does not cry "Look, ma, no hands"; she just leaves hands out of it. Her style has neither birthmarks nor those plaintive rebirthmarks, tattoos. Not that she disdains embellishment; in her there is nothing of unwashed Kate in burlap ("I am life"). Nor, on the other hand, is there anything of frilly femininity tendering little dainties from a fragile sensibility ("I am beauty," "I am feeling").

No-style means a general style, if we may risk such a term, a fusion of proved styles. She can do ordinary documentary whenever it is called for: the ship's passengers "advertised on little thumbtacked slips of paper that they had lost or found jeweled combs, down pillows, tobacco pouches, small cameras, pocket mirrors, rosaries." Here she sticks to nouns; yet she has no fear of the adjectives somewhat in disrepute now: "In the white heat of an early August morning a few placid citizens of the white-linen class strolled across the hard-baked surface of the public square under the dusty shade of the sweet-by-night trees. . . ." She relies without embarrassment on the plain, direct, ordinary, explicit. Veracruz "is a little purgatory"; Amparo decided "prematurely" that trouble was over. "Herr Lowenthal, who had been put at a small table by himself, studied the dinner card, with its list of unclean foods, and asked for a soft omelette with fresh green peas. He drank half a bottle of good wine to comfort himself. . . ."

On such sturdy foundations of style she can build in several ways. Without altering the everyday, matter-of-fact manner, she gets below the surface. Glocken, the hunchback, "scared people off; his plight was so obviously desperate they were afraid some of it would rub off on them." "Rub off": imaging casually a world of prophylactic finickiness. Captain Thiele paces the deck "alone, returning the respectful salutations of the passengers with reluctant little jerks of his head, upon which sat a monumental ornate cap, white as plaster." The commonplace comparison, dropped in without commotion at the end, unobtrusively deflates the large official figure. Of a shipboard communion service: "The priest went through the ceremony severely and hastily, placing the wafers on the outstretched tongues expertly and snatching back his hand." The plain adverbs suggest a minor public official in a distasteful routine: "snatch-ing," the fear of contamination. Mrs. Treadwell leaves a self-pitying young man: "If she stayed to listen, she knew she would weaken little by little, she would warm up in spite of herself, perhaps in the end identify herself with the other, take on his griefs and wrongs, and if it came to that, feel finally guilty as if she herself had caused them; yes, and he would believe it too, and blame her freely." The easy lucidity never shirks depths or darks, which to some writers seem approachable only by the involute, the cryptic, or the tortuous.

Using the kind of elements that she does, she can organize them, elaborately if need be, with control and grace. The local papers "cannot praise too much the skill with which the members of good society main-tain in their deportment the delicate balance between high courtesy and easy merriment, a secret of the Veracruz world bitterly envied and unsuc-cessfully imitated by the provincial inland society of the Capital." Under the gentle irony and the rhythm that serves it, lie in easy and well articulated orders a remarkable number of modifiers—such as Hardy would have fouled into knotty confusion, and James, pursuing precision, would have pried apart with preciosity in placement. She manages with equal skill the erection of ordinary terms, both concrete and analytical, into a periodic structure in which all elements converge unspectacularly on a climax of sudden insight: "The passengers, investigating the cramped airless quarters with their old-fashioned double tiers of bunks and a narrow hard couch along the opposite wall for the unlucky third comer, read the names on the doorplates—most of them German—eyed with suspicion and quick distaste luggage piled beside their own in their cabins, and each discovered again what he had believed lost for a while though he could not name it—his identity." A compact sketch of outer world and inner meaning, it is never crowded or awkward or rambling.

Language as guarantor of identity: it is the kind of true perception regularly conveyed in terms modest and unstraining, but fresh and compe-tent. Of the troubles of boarding ship: "This common predicament did not by any means make of them fellow sufferers." Each kept "his pride and separateness within himself"; "there crept into eyes meeting unwillingly . . . a look of unacknowledged, hostile recognition. 'So there you are again, I never saw you before in my life,' the eyes said." Of David Scott's special capacity for triumph as a lover: "Feeling within him his coldness of heart as a real power in reserve, he . . . laid his hand over hers warmly" —with just a shadow of oxymoron to accent the reality without calling attention to itself. Jenny Brown, his girl, had a "fondness for nearness, for stroking, touching, nestling, with a kind of sensuality so diffused it almost amounted to coldness after all": the plain tactile words preparing for the shrewd analysis in which the paradox is not thrust triumphantly at one but offered almost experimentally. There is a good deal of this relaxed movement between the physical and the psychic or moral, each grasped directly and surely. The Spanish dancers "would look straight at you and laugh as if you were an object too comic to believe, yet their eyes were cold and they were not enjoying themselves, even at your expense." The vocabulary is hardly more than elementary, and the words are arranged in a classic compound structure, almost as in an exercise book, yet they communicate a disturbing hardness. The next sentence is of the same stamp but is trimmed back sharply to an almost skeletal simplicity: "Frau Hutten had observed them from the first and she was afraid of them." The fear is ours, but not through a tensed-up stylistic staging of fear.

Miss Porter can combine words unexpectedly without becoming ostentatious: for instance, an adjective denoting mood or value with a neutral noun—"serious, well-shaped head," "weak dark whiskers," or, more urgently, "strong white rage of vengeful sunlight"; or sex words with gastric facts—"They fell upon their splendid full-bodied German food with hot appetites." She pairs partly clashing words: "softened and dispirited" (of a woman affected by childbirth), "with patience and a touch of severity" (of people waiting for the boat to leave), "oafish and devilish at once" (of a nagging inner voice), "at once crazed and stupefied" (of the air of a bad eating place): and gets inner contradictions in sharp phrases: "this pugnacious assertion of high breeding," "classic erotic-frowning smile" (of a dancer), "shameless pathos" (of an angry face). She can surprise, and convince, with a preposition: a newly married couple's "first lessons in each other."

She has strong, accurate, but not conspicuous, metaphors: "soggy little waiter," "pink-iced tea-cake of sympathy," "hand-decorated hates," "making conversation to scatter silence," a "laugh was a long cascade of falling tinware." But metaphors are less numerous than similes, that now less fashionable figure to which Miss Porter turns with instinctive ease, rarely without amplifying the sense or shading the tone, and always with the added thrust of imagistic vitality. She may fix the object visually: Elsa Lutz had a "crease of fat like a goiter at the base of the throat"; on her canvases Jenny Brown painted cubistic designs "in primary colors like fractured rainbows." She has a sense of how the inanimate may creep up on or take over the human: the steerage passengers "slept piled upon each other like dirty rags thrown out on a garbage heap"; or how a human attribute may be dehumanized: the Spanish dancers' voices "crashed like breaking crockery." When a woman, confident of her worldly knowingness, is publicly snubbed by the Captain, she first turns red; then her blush "vanished and left her pale as unborn veal"—colorless, unknowing, pre-innocent, pre-calf. When his wife bursts forth with a public expression of views contrary to his own, Professor Hutten "sat like something molded in sand, his expression that of a strong innocent man gazing into a pit of cobras." It is a complete picture of mood and man. Miss Porter confers her own incisive perception of character upon Jenny Brown when she has Jenny thinking about David Scott, ". . . I'll be carrying David like a petrified fetus for the rest of my life." Jenny's sense of rigidity and immaturity in her lover is really an echo of her creator's sense of many of her human subjects: she sees them with easy clarity and goes right to the point. Her images for them come solidly out of life; they are not stylistic gestures, literary exercises, but unlabored responses to need, responses from experience against which the door of feeling and knowing have never been closed.

The difficulty of describing a style without mannerisms, crotchets, or even characteristic brilliances or unique excellences leads one constantly to use such terms as *plain, direct, ordinary, unpretentious, lucid, candid.* These are neither derogatory nor limiting words, nor words that one is altogether content with. The qualities that they name are not inimical to the subtle or the profound, to the penetrating glance or the inclusive sweep. Whether Miss Porter's basic words are a multitude of documentary nouns or adjectives, are literally descriptive or pointedly or amplifyingly imagistic, are terms that report or present or comment or analyze, she composes them, without evident struggle, in a great variety of ways—in combinations of revelatory unexpectedness; tersely or compactly or with unencumbered elaboration, either in a succession of ordered dependencies or in structured periods where everything builds to a final emphasis; with an apparently automatic interplay of force and fluency; meticulously but not pickily or gracelessly; with a kind of graceful adjustment to situation that we call urbanity, yet by no means an urbanity that implies charm or agreeableness at the expense of firmness or conviction.

Certain of Miss Porter's arrangements disclose characteristic ways of perceiving and shaping her materials. She describes Veracruz as a "typical port town, cynical by nature, shameless by experience, hardened to showing its seamiest side to strangers: ten to one this stranger passing through is a sheep bleating for their shears, and one in ten is a scoundrel it would be a pity not to outwit." The traditional rhetoric—the triad series; the first half balanced against the second, which is balanced internally; the antithesis and chiasmus—is the instrument of clarity, analytical orderliness, and detachment. Miss Porter has a notable talent for the succinct summarizing sequence; she often employs the series, which combines specification with despatch; through it a packing together of near synonyms may master by saturation, or a quick-fingered catalogue may grasp a rush of simultaneous or consecutive events. A dancer's "pantomime at high speed" to an infatuated pursuer communicates "pity for him or perhaps his stupidity, contempt for the Lutzes, warning, insult, false commiseration, and finally, just plain ridicule." A series may define by a concise anatomy: William Denny's "mind seemed to run monotonously on women, or rather, sex; money, or rather his determination not to be gypped by anybody; and his health." Such series remind one of Jane Austen, who can often look at people and things as logically placeable, sometimes dismissable by a quick list of traits, or naturally amenable to a 1–2–3 kind of classification. Miss Porter has a marked Jane Austen side, which appears, for instance, in the dry summation of a girl and her parents: their "three faces were calm, grave, and much alike," with the anticlimax offhand instead of sharpened up into a shattering deflation. Miss Porter's comic sense is like Austen's both in the use of pithy geometrical arrangements and in the presentment of observed ironies, sometimes suffusing a whole scene, sometimes clipped down as in neoclassical verse: Elsa Lutz spoke "with a surprising lapse into everyday common sense" (cf. "But Shadwell seldom deviates into sense"); Herr Lowenthal felt "he was living in a world so dangerous he wondered how he dared go to sleep at night. But he was sleepy at that very moment." (cf. "And sleepless lovers, just at twelve, awake.") The irony is Austen-like when, though piercing, it is less censorious than tolerantly amused: "With relief he seized upon this common sympathy between them, and they spent a profitable few minutes putting the Catholic Church in its place." It may catch a social group, gently replacing the group's sense of itself by another: at the Captain's table Frau Rittersdorf "turned her most charming smile upon the Captain, who rewarded her with a glimpse of his two front teeth and slightly upturned mouthcorners. The others ranged round him, faces bent towards him like sunflowers to the sun, waiting for him to begin conversation." It may go beneath the surface to capture habits of mind, setting them up in a neat balance that comments on their insufficiency: Jenny Brown thinks wryly of " 'the family attitude'—suspicion of the worst based on insufficient knowledge of her life, and moral disapproval based firmly on their general knowledge of the weakness of human nature."

Yet to a passage with a strong Austen cast Miss Porter may make an inconspicuous addition that will elusively but substantially alter it. When Lizzi Spöckenkieker runs carelessly into pompous Captain Thiele, he "threw an arm about her stiffly," and she, "blushing, whinnying, cackling, scrambling, embraced him about the neck wildly as if she were drowning." There is the Austen series crisply hitting off the ludicrous behavior, but there is more visual imagery than Austen uses, more of the physically excessive, and "whinnying" and "cackling," dehumanizing words, carry the joke beyond the usual limit of the Austen mode. It is more like Charlotte Brontë, who could often plunge into the comic, but was likely to do it more fiercely and scornfully. With Brontë, the absurd more quickly edged into the grotesque and even the sinister; she had an awareness of potential damage not easily contained within a pure comic convention. Miss Porter is much closer to Brontë than to Austen in her description of Dr. Schumann when he catches the evil Spanish twins in another destructive practical joke: he "examined the depths of their eyes for a moment with dismay at their blind, unwinking malignance, their cold slyness—not beasts, though, but human souls."

Or consider this comment on a group of first-class passengers looking down on a steerage meal and feeling that the poor people there were being treated decently: "Murmuring among themselves like pigeons . . . [they] seemed to be vaguely agreed that to mistreat the poor is not right, and they would be the first to say so, at any time. Therefore they were happy to be spared this unpleasant duty, to have their anxieties allayed, their charitable feelings soothed." With the subdued ironic contemplation of the group, and with the series that dexterously encompasses their mood, this could be Austen's; and yet behind the smile-provoking self-deceit there is a kind of moral frailty, a trouble-breeding irresponsiblity, and in the steerage sights a degree of wretchedness, that extends beyond the borders of the comic perspective. Here, as elsewhere, Miss Porter's manner is reminiscent of George Eliot's—of a carefully, accurately analytical style that is the agent of a mature psychic and moral understanding. David Scott observes the non-dancers: "the born outsiders; the perpetual uninvited; the unwanted; and those who, like himself, for whatever sad reason, refused to join in." The series serves no comic end, speaks for no rationally organizing mind; it makes nice distinctions among the members of a class, somberly, with a mere touch of restrained sympathy to soften the categorical lines. Freytag mentally accuses boat travelers, who "can't seem to find any middle ground between stiffness, distrust, total rejection, or a kind of invasive, gnawing curiosity." The general precision is especially notable in the fresh, climactic joining of the learned "invasive" with the common "gnawing," the latter used uncharacteristically of an external trouble. There is an Eliot-like perceptiveness in Freytag's discovery "about most persons—that their abstractions and generalizations, their Rage for Justice or Hatred of Tyranny or whatever, too often disguised a bitter personal grudge of some sort far removed from the topic apparently under discussion" and in the matter-of-fact postscript that Freytag applied this only to others, never to himself. Miss Porter has repeated need for a vocabulary of emotional urgency, of tensions beyond comedy, as in Jenny Brown's concluding observation on the split with her family: "But that didn't keep you from loving them, nor them from loving you, with that strange longing, demanding, hopeless tenderness and bitterness, wound into each other in a net of living nerves." Here the terms for human contradictions are different in kind from those which present simply laughable incongruities. There is an Eliot note both in this and in another passage on the same page in which we are given a saddened sense of necessities which might, but does not, drift into bitterness: "She did not turn to them at last for help, or consolation, or praise, or understanding, or even love; but merely at last because she was incapable of turning away."

The language and syntax reveal Miss Porter's eye for precision, specification, and distinctions. There is the same precision in the definition of Freytag's "hardened expression of self-absorbed, accusing, utter righteousness" and of a stewardess's "unpleasant mixture of furtive insolence and false abasement, the all too familiar look of resentful servility." Freytag himself distinguishes the phases of another personality: "overfamiliar if you made the mistake of being pleasant to him; loud and insolent if he suspected timidity in you; sly and cringing if you knew how to put him in his place." David prefers, he thinks, "Mrs. Treadwell's unpretentious rather graceful lack of moral sense to Jenny's restless seeking outlaw nature trying so hard to attach itself to any or all points to the human beings nearest her: no matter who." Miss Porter confers her own flair for distinctions upon certain characters. Thus Dr. Schumann, planning to go to confession: ". . . he felt not the right contrition, that good habit of the spirit, but a personal shame, a crushing humiliation at the disgraceful nature of what he had to confess." And it is near the end of the book that Jenny, the most sentient and spontaneous character, reflects upon her griefs over love that did not fulfill expectations: "—and what had it been but the childish refusal to admit and accept on some term or other the difference between what one hoped was true and what one discovers to be the mere laws of the human condition?" The clarity in words comes here from the character's clarity of thought, and this in turn from the writer's clarity of mind. Thus an examination of style in the narrower sense of verbal deportment leads, as it repeatedly does, to the style in conceiving—to the "styling" of, we might say—episode and character, and from this on to the ultimate style of creative mind: the grasp of fact and the moral sense.

We have been following Miss Porter's range: from wit to wisdom, from the sense of the laughable slip or flaw to the awareness of graver self-deception and self-seeking, and to the feeling for reality that at once cuts through illusion and accepts, among the inevitable facts of life, the emotional pressures that lead to, and entangle, fulfillment and discord. Now beside this central sober work of reflective intelligence and alert conscience put the gay play of the Captain's being driven, by a "lethal cloud of synthetic rose scent" at dinner, to sneeze: "He sneezed three times inwardly, one forefinger pressed firmly to his upper lip as he had been taught to do in childhood, to avoid sneezing in church. Silently he was convulsed with internal explosions, feeling as if his eyeballs would fly out, or his eardrums burst. At last he gave up and felt for his handkerchief, sat up stiffly, head averted from the room, and sneezed steadily in luxurious agony a dozen times with muted sounds and streaming eyes, until the miasma was sneezed out and he was rewarded with a good nose-blow." This is farce, the comedy of the physical in which mind and feelings are engaged either not at all, or only mechanically: of the perversity of things and circumstances that render one absurd or grotesque with merely formal suffering, not the authentic kind that by stirring sympathy cuts off outrageous laughter. To say that it is in the vein of Smollett is to emphasize both its present rareness outside the work of committed funnymen and the extraordinariness of having it juxtaposed with writing of sensitiveness and thoughtfulness. Farce may have a satirical note, as in this note on Lizzi Spöckenkieker's disappointment with Herr Rieber, her would-be lover: "Every other man she had known had unfailingly pronounced the magic word *marriage* before ever he got into bed with her, no matter what came of it in fact." A little earlier, Herr Rieber, a short fat man, having gone through suitable amatory preliminaries, decided that his hour had come and, "with the silent intentness of a man bent on crime," maneuvered Lizzi, a tall thin woman, "to the dark side of the ship's funnel. He gave his prey no warning. . . . It was like embracing a windmill. Lizzi uttered a curious tight squeal, and her long arms gathered him in around his heaving middle. . . . She gave him a good push and they fell backward clutched together, her long active legs overwhelmed him, she rolled him over flat on his back, . . . Lizzi was spread upon him like a fallen tent full of poles. . . ." Herr Rieber's passion for flesh and conquest is defeated, turned into grief, by the vigorous surrender that has swept him into unorthodox subordination, and he can get rid of his victorious victim, who is in a "carnivorous trance," only by gasping to her in agony that they are watched by Bébé, that fat and generally seasick dog of Professor Hutten. Bebe, only three feet away, "the folds of his nose twitching, regarded them with an expression of animal cunning that most embarrassingly resembled human knowledge of the seamy side of life." After all the modern solemnities about sex, this sheer farce—with the farcical morality of the dog as grace censor—is reassuring evidence that a fuller, more flexible, less doleful sense of sexual conduct can be recovered.

For a final note on Miss Porter's great range, we can contrast this hilarious Smollettian jest with two quite dissimilar passages. One is the vivid imaging, in her visible gestures, of the inner unwellness of a Spanish countess: "Thumbs turned in lightly to the palm, the hands moved aimlessly from the edge of the table to her lap, they clasped and unclasped themselves, spread themselves flat in the air, closed, shook slightly, went to her hair, to the bosom of her gown, as if by a life of their own separate from the will of the woman herself, who sat quite still otherwise, features a little rigid, bending over to read the dinner card beside her plate." Though here there is a more detailed visualization of the symbolizing object, the feeling for the troubled personality is like Charlotte Brontë's. To this Countess, Dr. Schumann feels attracted, guiltily. After seeing her, "He lay down with his rosary in his fingers, and began to invite sleep, darkness, silence, that little truce of God between living and dying; he put out of his mind, with deliberate intention to forget forever, the last words of that abandoned lost creature; nettles, poisoned barbs, fish hooks, her words clawed at his mind with the terrible malignance of the devil-possessed, the soul estranged from its kind." In the meditative element, in the imaging of a remembered frenzy, and most of all in the particular moral sense that leads to the words "soul estranged from its kind," the account is reminiscent of Conrad.

Range means contrasts such as these. Often, too, there is direct juxtaposition of different styles. Miss Porter can write page after page of sonorous periods—plausible, not overplayed—for Professor Hutten's dinner disquisitions to a captive audience, and then shift bluntly to Frau Hutten's perspective: "He was boring them to death again, she could feel it like vinegar in her veins"—another trenchant simile. Here are two ways of commenting on intelligence: the cultivated irony of "[Elsa's] surprising lapse into everyday common sense," and, on the next page, Jenny's breezy colloquial hyperbole for the Cuban students, "The trouble . . . is simply that they haven't been born yet." David Scott solemnly claims a high disgust for sexual binges: "He had felt superior to his acts and to his partners in them, and altogether redeemed and separated from their vileness by that purifying contempt"; Jenny retorts, with pungent plainness, "Men love to eat themselves sick and then call their upchuck by high-sounding names." Or there is the innocent, flat-voiced irony of Miss Porter's comment on the "lyric prose" of newspapers reporting parties "lavish and aristocratic—the terms are synonymous, they believe" and on newly boarded passengers wandering "about in confusion with the air of persons who have abandoned something of great importance on shore, though they cannot think what it is"; and beside this the vulgar force appropriate to a tactical thought of Herr Rieber's: "A man couldn't be too cautious with that proper, constipated type, no matter how gamey she looked."

In their slangy vigor or insouciance, their blunt and easy immediacy, their spurning of the genteel, their casual clinicality, their nervous grip on strain and tension, some of these passages have an air that, whether in self-understanding or self-love, we call "modern." The novel has many such, and they evidence in another way the range of Miss Porter's style. However, the modernity need be stressed only enough to acknowledge that the style, like any well-wrought individual style, cannot be wholly placed by comparison with well-known styles. My principal points, nevertheless, have been that Miss Porter's style has strong affiliations with the Austen and Eliot styles, that its main lines are traditional rather than innovating, and that it is markedly devoid of namable singularities, mannerisms, private idioms, self-indulgent or striven-for uniquenesses that give a special coloration. These points are interrelated; to some extent, they are different emphases of a central truth.

To claim for a writer affinities with Austen and Eliot (and to note, as evidence of her variety, occasional reminiscences of other writers) may seem faint praise in an age quick to think, in many areas, we have left all that behind us. The procedure does have its risks, and a disavowal or two may be in order. To note a resemblance in styles is not to make premature judgments of over-all merit, which involves other problems not dealt with here, and which in the end must be left to history. It is not to suggest influences, imitation, idle repetition, failure of originality, or limitedness. On the contrary, it is a way of suggesting superiority in the individual achievement: here is a writer working independently, composing out of her own genius, and yet in her use of the language exhibiting admirable qualities that seem akin to those of distinguished predecessors. It is a way of proposing, perhaps, that she has got hold of some central virtues of the language, virtues whether of strength or grace, that tend to recur and that, whatever the modification of them from writer to writer, may in essence be inseparable from good writing. To say this is to imply a traditional style, or core of elements of style. To hypothesize a tradition is precarious, since the word seems likely to make critics either a bit solemn, seven-candled, and hieratic on the one hand, or, on the other, self-righteous, flambeaux-lighted, and rebellious with an anticlerical fervor. I venture the word, not to beg a theoretical issue or invoke a charm or scorn a curse, but to suggest figuratively a group of long-enduring ways of using the language, apparent norms of utility, representative workings-out of possibility. These would constitute a discipline of eccentricity but not a constraint on originality; to call a writer a traditionalist in style would involve the old paradox of unique personality seizing on the universal thing or mode.

It is in such terms that one must approach Miss Porter's style. Though it looks easy rather than hard, it has a certain elusiveness that makes it not quite easy to account for. It would be difficult to imitate or parody, for what is most open to copying or travestying is the novelty, the idiosyncrasy, the raw ego in words that betokens a flight from or an inability to get hold of some persisting "nature" in the art forms of one's own tongue. Miss Porter has a very wide vocabulary, but no pet vocabulary; she has considerable skill in compositional patterns but no agonized specializations of order. She is exact and explicit; she eschews mystery in the medium without losing the mystery in the matter. The solidity of her writing, of the *how* that implies the *what*, we signify by naming her peers. Her variety appears in an obviously wide spectrum of tones and attitudes, rarely with the pen as pardoner of all, or the stylus as stiletto, but within these extremes modulating easily among the contemptible, the laughable, the pitiable, the evasive laudable, and, most of all, the ever-present contradictory—of face and heart, belief and deed, illusion and fact—that regularly compels one to look anew at all familiar surfaces.

HOWARD MOSS

No Safe Harbor

Katherine Anne Porter's *Ship of Fools* (Atlantic-Little, Brown) is the story of a voyage—a voyage that seems to take place in many dimensions. A novel of character rather than of action, it has as its main purpose a study of the German ethos shortly before Hitler's coming to power in Germany. That political fact hangs as a threat over the entire work, and the novel does not end so much as succumb to a historical truth. But it is more than a political novel. *Ship of Fools* is also a human comedy and a moral allegory. Since its author commits herself to nothing but its top layer, and yet allows for plunges into all sorts of undercurrents, it is disingenuous to read on its surface alone and dangerous to read for its depths. Miss Porter has written one of those fine but ambiguous books whose values and meanings shift the way light changes as it passes through a turning prism.

Except for the embarkation at Veracruz and a few stopovers at ports, all the events occur aboard the *Vera*, a German passenger freighter, on its twenty-seven-day journey from Mexico to Germany in the summer of 1931. There is no lack of passengers; the cast is so immense that we are provided with not one but two keys at the beginning, so that we can keep the characters clearly in mind. The passenger list includes many Germans; a remarkable company of Spanish zarzuela singers and dancers—four men and four women—equally adept at performing, thieving, pimping, and whoring; the satanic six-year-old twins of two of the dancers, and four Americans: William Denny, a know-nothing chemical engineer from Texas; Mrs. Treadwell, a divorcée in her forties, who is constantly thwarted in

From *Writing Against Time: Critical Essays and Reviews.* Copyright © 1962 by Howard Moss. William Morrow & Company, Inc. Originally appeared in *The New Yorker.*

her attempts to disengage herself from the rest of the human race; and David Scott and Jenny Brown, two young painters who have been having an unhappy love affair for years, have never married, and quarrel end-lessly. There are also a Swede, some Mexicans, a Swiss innkeeper and his family, and some Cubans. The Germans are almost uniformly disagree-able—an arrogant widow, a windbag of a professor named Hutten, a violently anti-Semitic publisher named Rieber, a drunken lawyer, an Orthodox Jew who loathes Gentiles, a dying religious healer, and a hunchback, to name just a few. Each suffers from a mortal form of despair—spiritual, emotional, or religious. At Havana, La Condesa, a Spanish noblewoman who is being deported by the Cuban government, embarks, and so do eight hundred and seventy-six migrant workers, in steerage. They are being sent back to Spain because of the collapse of the Cuban sugar market.

In the little world of the *Vera*, plying across the ocean, the passengers become involved with one another not from choice but by proximity. Because of this, not very much happens, from the viewpoint of conventional drama. Miss Porter is interested in the interplay of character and not in the strategy of plotting. Her method is panoramic—cabin to cabin, deck to writing room, bridge to bar. She has helped herself to a device useful to a natural short-story writer: she manipulates one micro-cosm after another of her huge cast in short, swift scenes. Observed from the outside, analyzed from within, her characters are handled episodically. Place is her organizing element, time the propelling agent of her action. The *Vera* is a Hotel Universe always in motion.

As it proceeds, small crises blossom into odious flowers and expire. There are three major events. An oilman, Herr Freytag, a stainless Aryan, is refused the captain's table once it is learned that the wife he is going back to fetch from Germany is Jewish. A wood carver in steerage jumps overboard to save a dog thrown into the sea by the twins, and is drowned. And the zarzuela company arranges a costume-party "gala" whose ex-pressed purpose is to honor the captain but whose real motive is the fleecing of the other passengers. The characters, seeking release or support in one another, merely deepen each other's frustrations. Often these random associations end in violence—a violence always out of character and always revealing. Hansen, the Swede, who talks about a society in which the masses are not exploited, clubs the publisher with a beer bottle. The source of his immediate anger is his disappointed passion for one of the Spanish dancers. The funeral of the wood carver, the gentlest of men, becomes the occasion for a religious riot. Mrs. Treadwell, a carefully contained woman, well aware of the pointlessness and danger of meddling in other people's business, emerges from behind her bastion and beats up Denny in a drunken frenzy with the heel of a golden evening slipper.

If the relationships are not violent, they are damaging. Schumann, the ship's doctor, falling suddenly in love with the drug-addicted and possibly mad Condesa, risks his professional, spiritual, and emotional identity. The American painters hopelessly batter themselves in an affair they cannot resolve or leave alone. And the most solid of *Hausfraus*, Professor Hutten's wife, speaks up suddenly, as if against her will, to contradict her husband at the captain's table, an act doubly shameful for being public. Unable momentarily to put up with her husband's platitudes, to support a view of marriage she knows to be false, Frau Hutten, in her one moment of insight, undermines the only security she has. As character after character gives way to a compulsion he has been unaware of, it becomes evident why Miss Porter's novel is open to many interpretations. Through sheer accuracy of observation rather than the desire to demonstrate abstract ideas, she has hit upon a major theme: order vs. need, a theme observable in the interchange of everyday life and susceptible of any number of readings—political, social, religious, and psychological. Every major character is magnetized in time by the opposing forces of need and order. Mexico is the incarnation of need, Germany the representative of an order based on need. At the beginning, in Veracruz, there is a hideously crippled Mexican beggar, "dumb, half blind," who walks like an animal "following the trail of a smell." And the very last character in the book is a German boy in the ship's band, "who looked as if he had never had enough to eat in his life, nor a kind word from anybody," who "did not know what he was going to do next" and who "stared with blinded eyes." As the *Vera* puts in to Bremerhaven, he stands, "his mouth quivering while he shook the spit out of his trumpet, repeating to himself just above a whisper, 'Gruss Gott, Gruss Gott,' as if the town were a human being, a good and dear trusted friend who had come a long way to welcome him." Aboard the *Vera*, there is, on the one hand, the captain's psychotic authoritarianism, with its absolute and rigid standards of behavior, menaced always by human complexity and squalor; on the other, the Condesa's drug addiction and compulsion to seduce young men. Both are terrifying forms of fanaticism, and they complement each other in their implicit violence.

Dr. Schumann is the mediating agent between these two kinds of fanaticism. Suffering from a weak heart, he is going back to Germany—a Germany that no longer exists—to die. He is the product of a noble Teutonic strain, the Germany of intellectual freedom, scientific dispassion, and religious piety. He is a healer equally at home in the chaos of the steerage and in the captain's stateroom. But the Condesa shatters his philosophic detachment. He goes to her cabin at night and kisses her while she is asleep; he orders six young Cuban medical students to stay away from her cabin because he is jealous. Both acts are symptoms of a progressive desperation. First he refuses to express his need openly, out of fear; then he masks it by a display of authority. He becomes, finally, a conspirator in the Condesa's addiction. Since he is not able to separate the woman from the patient, in Dr. Schumann need and order become muddled. Mrs. Treadwell, an essentially sympathetic character, is drawn into Freytag's dilemma the same way—casually, then desperately. It is she who innocently tells her anti-Semitic cabinmate that Freytag's wife is Jewish, not knowing the information is meant to be confidential. He is bitter, forgetting that he has already blurted out the fact at the captain's table in a fit of anger and pride. Mrs. Treadwell wisely points out that his secret should never have been one in the first place. This is odd wisdom; Mrs. Treadwell has a few secrets of her own.

It is from such moral complications that the texture of *Ship of Fools* evolves—a series of mishaps in which both intention and the lack of intention become disasters. The tragedy is that even the best motive is adulterated when translated into action. Need turns people into fools, order into monsters. The *Vera's* first-class passengers stroll on deck gazing down into the abysmal pit of the steerage—pure need—just as they watch in envy the frozen etiquette of the captain's table and its frieze of simulated order. Even dowdy Frau Schmitt, a timid ex-teacher who cannot bear suffering in others, finally accepts the cruelty of Freytag's dismissal from the captain's table. If she does not belong there herself, she thinks, then where does she belong? A victim, she thus becomes a party to victimization—a situation that is to receive its perfect demonstration in the world of Nazi Germany, which shadows Miss Porter's book like a bird of carrion. Through the need to belong, the whole damaging human complex of fear, pride, and greed, a governing idea emerges from *Ship of Fools* that is rooted in the Prussian mystique of "blood and iron." It is the manipulation of human needs to conform to a version of order.

The flow of events in *Ship of Fools* is based on addiction (sex, drugs, food, and drink) or obsession (envy, pride, covetousness, and the rest). Yet even the most despicable characters, such as the Jew-hating Herr Rieber, seem surprisingly innocent. It is the innocence of ignorance, not of moral goodness. The humbug and misinformation exchanged between the passengers on the *Vera* are voluminous. Each person is trapped in that tiny segment of reality he calls his own, which he thinks about, and talks about, and tries to project to a listener equally obsessed. Not knowing who they are, these marathon talkers do not know the world they are capable of generating. Love is the sacrificial lamb of their delusions, and though it is pursued without pause, it is always a semblance, never a reality. Though they are terribly in need of some human connection, their humanity itself is in question.

Only the Spanish dancers seem to escape this fate. They transform need into a kind of order by subordinating it for financial gain or sexual pleasure, without involvement. They are comically and tragically evil; they have arranged a universe of money around sex and fraud. Consciously malignant, they are outdone by the natural malice of the twins, who throw the Condesa's pearls overboard in a burst of demoniacal spirits. The pearls are a prize the Spanish dancers had planned to steal. The evil of design is defeated by natural evil—a neat point. Even in this closed, diabolical society, in which the emotions have been disciplined for profit, the irrational disturbs the arrangement of things.

At one point, Jenny Brown recalls something she saw from a bus window when she was passing through a small Indian village in Mexico:

Half a dozen Indians, men and women, were standing together quietly in the bare spot near one of the small houses, and they were watching something very intently. As the bus rolled by, Jenny saw a man and a woman, some distance from the group, locked in a death battle. They swayed and staggered together in a strange embrace, as if they supported each other; but in the man's raised hand was a long knife, and the woman's breast and stomach were pierced. The blood ran down her body and over her thighs, her skirts were sticking to her legs with her own blood. She was beating him on the head with a jagged stone, and his features were veiled in rivulets of blood. They were silent, and their faces had taken on a saintlike patience in suffering, abstract, purified of rage and hatred in their one holy dedicated purpose to kill each other. Their flesh swayed together and clung, their left arms were wound about each other's bodies as if in love. Their weapons were raised again, but their heads lowered little by little, until the woman's head rested upon his breast and his head was on her shoulder, and holding thus, they both struck again.

It was a mere flash of visions, but in Jenny's memory it lived in an ample eternal day illuminated by a cruel sun.

This passage could be the center from which everything in Miss Porter's novel radiates. The human relations in it are nearly all reenacted counterparts of this silent struggle. Inside and out, the battle rages—the devout against the blasphemous, the Jew against the Gentile, class against class, nation against nation. The seemingly safe bourgeois marriages—of solid Germans, of stolid Swiss—are secret hand-to-hand combats. It is no better with lovers, children, and dogs. The dog thrown into the sea by the evil twins is at least rescued by the good wood carver before he drowns. But on the human level the issues are obscure, the colors blurred; the saint is enmeshed with the devil. Struggling to get at the truth—*Vera* means "true" in Latin—the passengers in *Ship of Fools* justify its title. What truth is there for people who must lie in order to exist, Miss Porter seems to be asking. Against her insane captain and her mad Condesa, Miss Porter poses only the primitive and the remote—an enchanting Indian servant aboard ship, the appearance of three whales, a peasant woman nursing a baby. They are as affecting as a silence in nature.

Miss Porter is a moralist, but too good a writer to be one except by implication. Dogma in *Ship of Fools* is attached only to dogmatic characters. There is not an ounce of weighted sentiment in it. Its intelligence lies not in the profundity of its ideas but in the clarity of its viewpoint; we are impressed not by what Miss Porter says but by what she knows. Neither heartless nor merciful, she is tough. Her virtue is disinterestedness, her strength objectivity. Her style is free of displays of "sensitivity," musical effects, and interior decoration. Syntax is the only instrument she needs to construct an enviable prose. But the book differs from her extraordinary stories and novellas in that it lacks a particular magic she has attained so many times on a smaller scale. The missing ingredient is impulse. *Ship of Fools* was twenty years in the writing; the stories read as if they were composed at one sitting, and they have the spontaneity of a running stream. *Ship of Fools* is another kind of work—a summing up, not an overflowing—and it is devoid of one of the excitements of realistic fiction. The reader is never given that special satisfaction of the drama of design, in which the strings, having come unwound, are ultimately tied together in a knot. Miss Porter scorns patness and falseness, but by the very choice of her method she also lets go of suspense. She combines something of the intellectual strategy of Mann's *Magic Mountain* (in which the characters not only are themselves but represent ideas or human qualities) with the symbolic grandeur of *Moby Dick* (in which a predestined fate awaits the chief actors). Her goodbye to themes of Mexico and Germany (two subjects that have occupied her elsewhere) is a stunning farewell, but it lacks two components usually considered essential to masterpieces—a hero and a heroic extravagance.

Ship of Fools is basically about love, a human emotion that teeters helplessly between need and order. On the *Vera's* voyage there is precious little of it. The love that comes too late for the Condesa and Dr. Schumann is the most touching thing in it. But the Condesa is deranged, ill, and exiled; the dying Doctor is returning to a Germany that has vanished.

The one true example of love—a pair of Mexican newlyweds—is never dwelt upon. We are left with this image of two people, hand in hand, who have hardly said a word in all the thousands that make up Miss Porter's novel. In *Ship of Fools*, every human need but one is exposed down to its nerve ends. Love alone remains silent, and abstract.

EUDORA WELTY

The Eye of the Story

In "Old Mortality" how stirring the horse race is! At the finish the crowd breaks into its long roar "like the falling walls of Jericho." This we hear, and it is almost like seeing, and we know Miss Lucy has won. But beyond a fleeting glimpse—the "mahogany streak" of Miss Lucy on the track—we never get much sight of the race with our eyes. What we see comes afterward. Then we have it up close: Miss Lucy bleeding at the nose. For Miranda has got to say "That's winning too." The race would never have got into the story except that Miranda's heart is being prepared to reject victory, to reject the glamor of the race and the cheering grandstand; to distrust from now on all evidence except what she, out of her own experience, can testify to. By the time we *see* Miss Lucy, she is a sight for Miranda's eyes alone: as much symbol as horse.

Most good stories are about the interior of our lives, but Katherine Anne Porter's stories take place there; they show surface only at her choosing. Her use of the physical world is enough to meet her needs and no more; she is not wasteful with anything. This artist, writing her stories with a power that stamps them to their last detail on the memory, does so to an extraordinary degree without sensory imagery.

I have the most common type of mind, the visual, and when first I began to read her stories it stood in the way of my trust in my own certainty of what was there that, for all my being bowled over by them, I couldn't see them happening. This was a very good thing for me. As her work has done in many other respects, it has shown me a thing or two about the eye of fiction, about fiction's visibility and invisibility, about its clarity, its radiance.

From *The Yale Review* (December 1965). Copyright © 1965 by Eudora Welty.

Heaven knows she can see. Katherine Anne Porter has seen all her life, sees today, most intimately, most specifically, and down to the bones, and she could date the bones. There is, above all, "Noon Wine" to establish it forever that when she wants a story to be visible, it is. "Noon Wine" is visible all the way through, full of scenes charged with dramatic energy; everything is brought forth into movement, dialogue; the title itself is Mr. Helton's tune on the harmonica. "Noon Wine" is the most beautifully objective work she has done. And nothing has been sacrificed to its being so (or she wouldn't have done it); to the contrary. I find Mr. Hatch the scariest character she ever made, and he's just set down there in Texas, like a chair. There he stands, part of the everyday furniture of living. He's opaque, and he's the devil. Walking in at Mr. Thompson's gate—the same gate by which his tracked-down victim walked in first—he is that much more horrifying, almost too solid to the eyes to be countenanced. (So much for the visual mind.)

Katherine Anne Porter has not in general chosen to cast her stories in scenes. Her sense of human encounter is profound, is fundamental to her work, I believe, but she has not often allowed it the dramatic character it takes in "Noon Wine." We may not see the significant moment happen within the story's present; we may not watch it occur between the two characters it joins. Instead, a silent blow falls while one character is alone—the most alone in his life, perhaps. (And this is the case in "Noon Wine" too.) Often the revelation that pierces a character's mind and heart and shows him his life or his death comes in a dream, in retrospect, in illness or in utter defeat, the moment of vanishing hope, the moment of dying. What Miss Porter makes us see are those subjective worlds of hallucination, obsession, fever, guilt. The presence of death hovering about Granny Weatherall she makes as real and brings as near as Granny's own familiar room that stands about her bed—realer, nearer, for we recognize not only death's presence but the character death has come in for Granny Weatherall.

The flash of revelation is revelation but is unshared. But how unsuspecting we are to imagine so for a moment—it *is* shared, and by ourselves, her readers, who must share it feeling the doubled anguish of knowing this fact, doubled still again when it is borne in upon us how close to life this is, to *our* lives.

It is to be remembered that the world of fiction is not of itself visible. A story may or may not be born in sensory images in a given writer's mind. Experience itself is stored in no telling how many ways in a writer's memory. (It was "the sound of the sea, and Beryl fanning her hair at the window" that years later and thousands of miles away brought

Katherine Mansfield to writing "At the Bay.") But if the physical world *is* visible or audible in the story, it has to be made so. Its materialization is as much a created thing as are the story's characters and what they think or do or say.

Katherine Anne Porter shows us that we do not have to see a story happen to know what is taking place. For all we are to know, she is not looking at it happen herself when she writes it; for her eyes are always looking through the gauze of the passing scene, not distracted by the immediate and transitory; her vision is reflective.

Her imagery is as likely as not to belong to a time other than the story's present, and beyond that it always differs from it in nature; it is *memory* imagery, coming into the story from memory's remove. It is a distilled, a re-formed imagery, for it is part of a language made to speak directly of premonition, warning, surmise, anger, despair.

It was soon borne in upon me that Katherine Anne Porter's moral convictions have given her readers another way to see. Surely these convictions represent the fixed points about which her work has turned, and not only that but they govern her stories down to the smallest detail. Her work has formed a constellation, with its own North Star.

Is the writer who does not give us the pictures and bring us the sounds of a story as it unfolds shutting out part of life? In Katherine Anne Porter's stories the effect has surely been never to diminish life but always to intensify life in the part significant to her story. It is a darkening of the house as the curtain goes up on this stage of her own.

Her stories of Mexico, Germany, Texas all happen there: where love and hate, trust and betrayal happen. And so their author's gaze is turned not outward but inward, and has confronted the mysterious dark from her work's beginning.

Since her subject is what lies beneath the surface, her way—quite direct—is to penetrate, brush the stuff away. It is the writer like Chekov whose way of working is indirect. He moved indeed toward the same heart and core but by building up some corresponding illusion of life. Writers of Chekov's side of the family are themselves illusionists and have necessarily a certain fondness for, lenience toward, the whole shimmering fabric as such. Here we have the professional scientist, the good doctor, working with illusion and the born romantic artists—is she not?—working without it. Perhaps it is always the lyrical spirit that takes on instantaneous color, shape, pattern of motion in work, while the mediative spirit must fly as quickly as possible out of the shell.

All the stories she has written are moral stories about love and the hate that is love's twin, love's imposter and enemy and death. Rejection, betrayal, desertion, theft roam the pages of her stories as they roam the world. The madam kicking the girl in "Magic" and the rest of the brutality in the characters' treatment of one another; the thieving that in one form or another infects their relationships; the protests they make, from the weakness of false dreams or of lying down with a cold cloth over the eyes, on up to towering rages: all this is a way of showing to the inward eye: Look at what you are doing to human love.

We hear in how many more stories than the one the litany of the little boy at the end of "The Downward Path to Wisdom," his "comfortable, sleepy song": "I hate Papa, I hate Mama, I hate Grandma, I hate Uncle David, I hate Old Janet, I hate Marjory, I hate Papa, I hate Mama. . . ." It is like the long list of remembered losses in the story "Theft" made vocal, and we remember how that loser's decision to go on and let herself be robbed coincides with the rising "in her blood" of "a deep almost murderous anger."

"If one is afraid of looking into a face one hits the face," remarked W. B. Yeats, and I think we must conclude that to Katherine Anne Porter's characters this face is the challenging face of love itself. And I think it is the faces—the inner, secret faces—of her characters, in their self-delusion, their venom and pain, that their author herself is contemplating. More than either looking at the face or hitting it, she has made a story out of her anger.

If outrage is the emotion she has most strongly expressed, she is using outrage as her cool instrument. She uses it with precision to show what monstrosities of feeling come about not from the lack of the existence of love but from love's repudiation, betrayal. From which there is no safety anywhere. Granny Weatherall, eighty, wise, affectionate and good, and now after a full life dying in her bed with the priest beside her, "knew hell when she saw it."

The anger that speaks everywhere in the stories would trouble the heart for their author whom we love except that her anger is pure, the reason for it evident and clear, and the effect exhilarating. She has made it the tool of her work; what we do is rejoice in it. We are aware of the compassion that guides it, as well. Only compassion could have looked where she looks, could have seen and probed what she sees. Real compassion is perhaps always in the end unsparing; it must make itself a part of knowing. Self-pity does not exist here; these stories come out trenchant, bold, defying; they are tough as sanity, unrelinquished sanity, is tough.

Despair is here, as well described as if it were Mexico. It is a despair, however, that is robust and sane, open to negotiation by the light of day. Life seen as a savage ordeal has been investigated by a straightforward courage, unshaken nerve, a rescuing wit, and above all with the searching intelligence that is quite plainly not to be daunted. In the end the stories move us not to despair ourselves but to an emotion quite opposite because they are so seriously and clear-sightedly pointing out what they have been formed to show: that which is true under the skin, that which will remain a fact of the spirit.

Miranda, by the end of "Old Mortality" rebelling against the ties of the blood, resenting their very existence, planning to run away now from these and as soon as she can from her own escape into marriage, Miranda saying "I hate loving and being loved," is hating what destroys loving and what prevents being loved. She is, in her own particular and her own right, fighting back at the cheat she has discovered in all that's been handed down to her as gospel truth.

Seeing what is not there, putting trust in a false picture of life, has been one of the worst nightmares that assail her characters. "My dreams never renege on me, Mr. Richards. They're all I have to go by," says Rosaleen. (The Irish are no better than the Southerners in this respect.) Not only in the comic and touching Rosaleen, the lovely and sentient and tragic Miranda, but in many other characters throughout the stories we watch the romantic and the anti-romantic pulling each other to pieces. Is the romantic ever scotched? I believe not. Even if there rises a new refrain, even if the most ecstatic words ever spoken turn out to be "I hate you," the battle is not over for good. That battle is in itself a romance.

Nothing is so naturally subject to false interpretation as the romantic, and in furnishing that interpretation the Old South can beat all the rest. Yet some romantic things happen also to be true. Miss Porter's stories are not so much a stand against the romantic as such, as a repudiation of the false. What alone can instruct the heart is the experience of living, experience which can be vile; but what can never do it any good, what harms it more than vileness, are those tales, those legends of more than any South, those universal false dreams, the hopes sentimental and ubiquitous, which are not on any account to be gone by.

For there comes a confrontation. It is then that Miss Porter's characters, behaving so entirely like ourselves, make the fatally wrong choice. Enter betrayal. Again and again, enter betrayal. We meet the betrayal that lies in rejection, in saying No to others or No to the self, or that lies with still more cunning in saying Yes when this time it should have been No.

And though we are all but sure what will happen, we are possessed by suspense.

It appears to me irrelevant whether or not the story is conceived and put down in sensory images, whether or not it is dramatic in construction, so long as its hold is a death-grip. In my own belief, the suspense—so acute and so real—in Katherine Anne Porter's work never did depend for its life on disclosure of the happenings of the narrative (nothing is going to turn out very well) but in the writing of the story, which becomes one single long sustained moment for the reader. Its suspense is one with its meaning. It must arise, then, from the mind, heart, spirit by which it moves and breathes.

It is a current like a strand of quicksilver through the serenity of her prose. In fiction of any substance, serenity can only be an achievement of the work itself, for any sentence that is alive with meaning is speaking out of passion. Serenity never belonged to the *now* of writing; it belongs to the later *now* offered its readers. In Katherine Anne Porter's work the forces of passion and self-possession seem equal, holding each other in balance from one moment to the next. The suspense born of the writing abides there in its own character, using the story for its realm, a quiet and well-commanded suspense, but a genie.

There was an instinct I had, trustworthy or not, that the matter of visibility in her stories had something to do with time. Time permeates them. It is a grave and formidable force.

Ask what time it is in her stories and you are certain to get the answer: the hour is fateful. It is not necessary to see the hands of the clock in her work. It is a time of racing urgency, and it is already too late. And then recall how many of her characters are surviving today only for the sake of tomorrow, are living on tomorrow's coming; think how we see them clearest in reference to tomorrow. Granny Weatherall, up to the last—when God gives her no sign acceptable to her and jilts her Himself—is thinking: "There was always so much to be done, let me see: tomorrow." Laura in "Flowering Judas" is "waiting for tomorrow with a bitter anxiety as if tomorrow may not come." Ordinary, self-respecting, and—up to a certain August day—fairly well blessed Mr. Thompson, because he has been the one to kill the abominable Mr. Hatch, is self-tried, self-pleaded for, and self-condemned to no tomorrow; neither does he leave his sons much of a tomorrow, and certainly he leaves still less of one to poor, red-eyed Mrs. Thompson, who had "so wanted to believe that tomorrow, or at least the day after, life, such a battle at best, was going to be better." In "Old Mortality" time takes Miranda by the hand and leads her into promising herself "in her hopefulness, her ignorance": "At least I can know the truth about what happens to me." In "Pale Horse, Pale Rider" the older Miranda asks Adam, out of her suffering, "Why can we not save each other?" and the straight answer is that there is no time. The story ends with the unforgettable words "Now there would be time for everything" because tomorrow has turned into oblivion, the ultimate betrayer is death itself.

But time, one of the main actors in her stories—teacher, fake healer, conspirator in betrayal, ally of death—is also, within the complete control of Miss Porter, with his inimical powers made use of, one of the movers of her writing, a friend to her work. It occurred to me that what is *seeing* the story is the dispassionate eye of time. Her passionate mind has asked itself, schooled itself, to use Time's eye. Perhaps Time is the genie's name.

Laura is stuck in time, we are told in "Flowering Judas"—and told in the timeless present tense of dreaming, a brilliant working upon our very nerves to let us know precisely Laura's dilemma. There is in all Katherine Anne Porter's work the strongest sense of unity in all the parts; and if it is in any degree a sound guess that an important dramatic element in the story has another role, a working role, in the writing of the story, might this not be one source of a unity so deeply felt? Such a thing in the practice of an art is unsurprising. Who can separate a story from the story's writing?

And there is too, in all the stories, a sense of long, learning life, the life that is the story's own, beginning from a long way back, extending somewhere into the future. As we read, the initial spark is not being struck before our eyes; the fire we see has already purified its nature and burns steadied by purpose, unwavering in meaning. It is no longer impulse, it is a signal, a beacon.

To me, it is the image of the eye of time that remains the longest in the mind at her story's end. There is a judgment to be passed. A moral judgment has to be, in all reason, what she has been getting at. But in a still further act of judiciousness, I feel, she lets Time pass that judgment.

Above all, I feel that what we are responding to in Katherine Anne Porter's work is the intensity of its life, which is more powerful and more profound than even its cry for justice.

They are excoriating stories. Does she have any hope for us at all? Well, do we not feel its implication everywhere—a desperate hope for the understanding that may come, if we use great effort, out of tomorrow, or if not then, maybe the day after? Clearly it has to become at some point an act of faith. It is toward this that her stories all point: here, it seems to me, is the North Star.

And how calm is the surface, the invisible surface of it all! In a style as invisible as the rhythm of a voice, and as much her own as her own voice, she tells her stories of horror and humiliation and in the doing fills her readers with a rising joy. The exemplary prose that is without waste or extravagance or self-indulgence or display, without any claim for its triumph, is full of pride. And her reader shares in that pride, as well he might: it is pride in the language, pride in using the language to search out human meanings, pride in the making of a good piece of work. A personal spell is about the stories, the something of her own that we refer to most often, perhaps, when we mention its beauty, and I think this comes from the *making* of the stories.

Readers have long been in the habit of praising (or could it be at times reproaching?) Katherine Anne Porter by calling her a perfectionist. I do not agree that this is the highest praise, and I would think the word misleading, suggesting as it does in the author a personal vanity in technique and a rigidity, even a deadness, in her prose. To me she is something more serious than a perfectionist. I celebrate her for being a blessed achiever. First she is an artist, of course, and as an artist she is an achiever.

That she hasn't wasted precious time repeating herself in her stories is sign enough, if it were needed, that she was never interested in doing the thing she knew already that she was able to bring off, that she hasn't been showing off for the sake of high marks (from whom?), but has patiently done what was to her her born necessity, quietly and in her own time, and each time the way she saw fit.

We are left with a sense of statement. Virginia Woolf set down in her diary, on the day when she felt she had seen that great brave difficult novel *The Waves* past a certain point in the writing: "But I think it possible that I have got my statues against the sky." It is the achieving of this crucial, this monumental moment in the work itself that we feel has mattered to Katherine Anne Porter. The reader who looks for the flawless result can find it, but looking for that alone he misses the true excitement, exhilaration, of reading, of rereading. It is the achieving—in a constant present tense—of the work that shines in the mind when we think of her name; and in that achieving lies, it seems to me, the radiance of the work and our recognition of it as unmistakably her own.

And unmistakable is its source. Katherine Anne Porter's deep sense of fairness and justice, her ardent conviction that we need to give and to receive in loving kindness all the human warmth we can make— here is where her stories come from. If they are made by the mind and address the mind, they draw their eloquence from a passionate heart. And for all their pain, they draw their wit, do they not, from a reserve of natural gayety? I have wondered before now if it isn't those who were born gay who can devote themselves most wholeheartedly in their work to seriousness, who have seriousness to burn. The gay are the rich in feeling, and don't need to save any of it back.

Unmistakable, too, is what this artist has made. Order and form no more spring out of order and form than they come riding in to us upon seashells through the spray. In fiction they have to be made out of their very antithesis, life. The art of making is the thing that has meaning, and I think beauty is likely to be something that has for a time lain under good, patient hands. Whether the finished work of art was easy or hard to make, whether it demanded a few hours or many years, concerns nobody but the maker, but the making itself has shaped that work for good and all. In Katherine Anne Porter's stories we feel their making as a bestowal of grace.

It is out of the response to her particular order and form that I believe I may have learned the simplest and surest reason for why I cannot see her stories in their every passing minute, and why it was never necessary or intended that a reader should. Katherine Anne Porter is writing stories of the spirit, and the time that fills those moments is eternity.

M.M. LIBERMAN

Symbolism, the Short Story, and "Flowering Judas"

The short story is not quite a poem any more than it is a short novel boiled conveniently down to bite size. So it cannot, therefore, be done with sounds, sights, and symbols alone. Surely he was correct who contended that "the storyteller must have a story to tell, not merely some sweet prose to take out for a walk." And so was that editor who wrote to Katherine Anne Porter, "No plot, my dear, no story," although how he supposed that stricture to apply to *her* work I can imagine only in a way that does him no credit.

Commentators and editors have grouped Miss Porter's stories in a variety of ways: early—late, Miranda—Laura, new order—old order, and Mexican—non-Mexican, to name a few. This habit is conventional and usually harmless enough; it does not mislead if one keeps in mind that it is usually more a descriptive than a critical practice. It is more to the point of criticism, however, to see a "story" as falling naturally into two groups which are explicitly evaluative according to degree of formal accomplishment: realized stories with sufficient verbal efficacy to compensate adequately for the absence of the explicit causal-temporal logic essential only to most longer fictional forms; and alleged stories which no amount of verbal magic can rescue from a poverty of implied plot and other indispensable narrative features.

"During the 1940's, it was as symbolist that Miss Porter was most effusively praised by totemist critics," James William Johnson reminds us. "In fact, criticism of her work became tantamount to an intellectual parlor game: 'Let's see who can find the most abstruse symbols in "Flowering Judas." ' Her work survived this craze, which was largely unnecessary, since the truth is that her symbols operate on the most direct level and, where she intends a multiplicity of meaning, Miss Porter almost always tells the reader so." It ought to be added to Mr. Johnson's refreshingly common-sensical observation that although her work has survived "this craze," the "craze" itself dies hard. The neo-euhemerism of the thirties and forties seems down but by no means out, and the readings of "Flowering Judas" which can serve as paradigms of that era's notorious and, often, hilarious symbol-mongering have, to my knowledge, never been recanted. More-over, the epigones of the totemists are still publishing critiques of Miss Porter's stories founded on the assumption that there is nothing, given sufficient ingenuity, that cannot be read as metaphysical verse.

"Flowering Judas" is, to be sure, a highly figurative composition. The modern short story almost invariably is, because, perhaps paradoxi-cally, its author is likely to write in a realistic mode. For whereas the publicly verifiable in the novel requires extended treatment, partly in order to represent time sequentially, the familiar in the short story, dealing as it does with the moment, can be represented best by a good deal of shorthand. The result has been a "symbolic realism" where the most ordinary events are imitated, but by a selective process so scrupulous as to evoke at least what the novel might show or tell. When most successful, as in "Flowering Judas," the evocations are practically symbolic in that they stand for more than themselves. It follows that, mistaking the means for the end, the amateur is forever producing the unwritten. In the place of the authentic story there is fobbed off something between an impressionistic hodgepodge and a bastard lyric, known at times as the "mood piece" and at others as the "prose poem." There is also the "slice-of-life," and, more recently, the "open-ended" story, a legitimate enough form, if it is not open at both ends, top and bottom. Since on the contrary "Flowering Judas" is so plainly a fully realized effort to tell a tale classically, that is, to move a serious theme through implied time by means of characters who act on ethical choices, and to do this, moreover, without failing to accommodate to theme, wherever possible, the details of image and fable, it might, therefore, be wise to be a bit warier than most critics have been of reading this story as if its meaning partook of its figuration rather than, as I believe to be the case, the reverse.

There has been no slackening of published interest in "Flowering Judas," but the standard reading continues to be the West-Stallman analy-sis which appeared in a college anthology of short fiction in 1949. I know of no reading that does not take off from it, at least in its basic assumption of the accessibility of theme and meaning through symbolism. The text is incorrectly titled "The Flowering Judas." If one believed that the causes of error are unconscious but real, the accident would be seen as a true mistake. For West and Stallman, *the* flowering Judas is virtually *the* story. The analysis itself is titled "Theme through Symbol," which, I contend, is not a viable concept for narrative fiction. The West-Stallman reading asks what the purpose of the individual symbol is, and replies that it is to "signify the theme." "In the title itself" the "most important" symbol "occurs," and the source is given as Eliot's "Gerontion." "This is scarcely a coincidence," we are told, "since Eliot's passage so clearly suggests Laura's activity at the end of the story." The five lines in which the words "flowering Judas" appear are quoted as if they are proof. The Judas tree is seen quite simply as "a symbol for the betrayer of Christ." Laura's eating the buds is a "sacrament . . . of betrayal." If we put aside the question of failure to cite evidence of Miss Porter's specific debt to Eliot in this instance, we are nonetheless free to grant her known interest in Eliot and the obviousness of the betrayal theme in both poem and story do, admittedly, constitute presumptive evidence of source. But to go further in lining up the story with the poem is to jump to conclusions about the use of the symbol, based mistakenly on the assumption that symbols are used in stories quite as they might be in poems, that is, to signify theme. In fact, in Miss Porter's story, the symbol of the flowering Judas is employed to enhance theme and finally to reiterate theme, but not to be a sign of theme as if theme had not been established by other means. Laura is found wanting from beginning to end, and the meaning of the story does not wait on a final symbolic revelation to make accessible what would otherwise be mysterious. "I have a great deal of religious symbolism in my stories," Miss Porter recently allowed, "because I have a very deep sense of religion and also I have a religious training. And I suppose you don't invent symbolism. You don't say, 'I'm going to have the flowering Judas tree stand for betrayal,' but of course it does." Of course, it does, because given the association of the name Judas it can. But it does only if the author, in effect, employs it to that end. If the reader can recognize the Judas tree as a symbol of betrayal, he can do so legitimately, and not arbitrarily, only if he has been permitted to see betrayal in the story's action. It is the story, all in all, that makes of this particular tree a working symbol of anything whatever. In a work as psychologically realistic as this one, concerned as it is with the levels of a young woman's harassed consciousness (Laura's mind is in fact the work's arena), the Judas tree does not stand primarily and independently as the figure of pagan treachery, analogous to Laura's treachery. Rather it illuminates, dream image that it is, the natural depths of the bedeviled feelings of a woman who cannot, when awake, come to terms with those feelings. Seen this way, "Flowering Judas" is not a symbolic story in the sense that it depends on symbols to pull its thematic irons out of the fire. The entire work is in a way "symbolic" insofar as it impels the reader to attend to one striking detail and not another. But within this sense of symbol the Judas tree as a figure is not the most important. It cannot, logically, be more important than any other narrative detail which gives us insight into Laura's character. It may seem crucial because of its strategic location, that is, at the end. Thus placed, however, it can astonish only a reader who has paid little attention to the work's beginning, as might astonish the figurative phrase "my eyes burned" at the conclusion of Joyce's "Araby," a story which begins, "North Richmond Street, being blind, was a quiet street. . . ."

Miss Porter has written of "Flowering Judas":

> All the characters and episodes are based on real persons and events, but naturally, as my memory worked upon them and time passed, all assumed different shapes and colors, formed gradually around a central idea, that of self-delusion, the order and meaning of the episodes changed, and became in a word fiction.
>
> The idea first came to me one evening when going to visit the girl I call Laura in the story, I passed the open window of her living room on my way to the door, through the small patio which is one of the scenes in the story. I had a brief glimpse of her sitting with an open book in her lap, but not reading, with a fixed look of pained melancholy and confusion in her face. The fat man I call Braggioni was playing the guitar and singing to her.
>
> In that glimpse, no more than a flash, I thought I understood, or perceived, for the first time, *the desperate complications of her mind* and feelings, and I knew a story; perhaps not her true story, not even the real story of the whole situation, but all the same a story that seemed *symbolic truth* to me. If I had not seen her face at the very moment, I should never have written just this story because I should not have known it to write [italics mine].

"Flowering Judas" owes its greatness not at all to some opportunistic employment of a conventional religious symbol to signify theme but to a brilliant narrative practice throughout, one capable of representing a feeling that, once apprehended by the reader, permits him to see with what overriding intelligence Miss Porter knew her Laura, "the desperate complications of her mind" and what it meant.

The celebrated dream sequence on which the story ends and which is supposed to be central in its resolution and revelation through the symbol of the tree and the buds follows:

The tolling of the midnight bell is a signal, but what does it mean? Get up, Laura, and follow me: come out of your sleep, out of your bed, out of this strange house. What are you doing in this house? Without a word, without fear she rose and reached for Eugenio's hand, but he eluded her with a sharp sly smile and drifted away. This is not all, you shall see—Murderer, he said, follow me, I will show you a new country, but it is far away and we must hurry. No, said Laura, not unless you take my hand, no; and she clung first to the stair rail and then to the topmost branch of the Judas tree that bent down slowly and set her upon the earth, and then to the rocky ledge of a cliff, and then to the jagged wave of a sea that was not water but a desert of crumbling stone. Where are you taking me, she asked in wonder but without fear. To death, and it is a long way off, and we must hurry, said Eugenio. No, said Laura, not unless you take my hand. Then eat these flowers, poor prisoner, said Eugenio in a voice of pity, take and eat: and from the Judas tree he stripped the warm bleeding flowers, and held them to her lips. She saw that his hand was fleshless, a cluster of small white petrified branches, and his eye sockets were without light, but she ate the flowers greedily for they satisfied both hunger and thirst. Murderer! said Eugenio, and Cannibal! This is my body and my blood. Laura cried No! and at the sound of her own' voice, she awoke trembling, and was afraid to sleep again.

It has been prepared for by a single reference to the Judas tree earlier in connection with a "brown, shock-haired youth" who pleaded for her love in vain. Laura, for her part, "could think of nothing to do about it."

The sense one gets of Laura's emotional stinginess is not so much that, Judas-like, she has betrayed the young man in withholding human warmth but that, like the central figure of "Theft," Miss Porter's story of another young woman who is seen explicitly to have stolen life's spiritual riches from *herself*, Laura has betrayed Laura. We know next to nothing of the young man, but we know how desperately Laura needs to fulfill herself. The young man will fare badly, but it is not inevitable. Laura, on the other hand, is doomed forever to suffer her own starving soul, a fact confirmed by a negation and fear of life and truth, the note on which the very last image is played out. But nothing of what is given to the reader anywhere in the dream sequence is unprepared for, and is, moreover, explicitly *reasoned* by the narrator the moment it is possible to intrude sufficiently to explain Laura. In a work of fiction in which the narrator tells the reader what he needs to know, no symbol so arbitrary as to liken a frightened nunlike girl to the historical Judas is artistically allowable. Nor is Miss Porter guilty of such faulty aesthetic judgment.

If Miss Porter is a symbolist only in the sense we have described, that is, as a writer whose choices of vocabulary, of levels of diction, and of varieties of image work insistently to induce one to read beyond mere denotation, she is also a symbolist in "Flowering Judas" in the sense of her own phrase "symbolic truth," which I take to be synonymous with "meaning."

Finally, the West-Stallman reading has it that:

> Laura is not redeemed, even though she desires it, as the eating of the buds of the Judas tree suggests. Her sacrament is a devouring gesture and Eugenio calls her a cannibal, because she is devouring him (Man). She is, like Judas, the betrayer—the destroyer; and her betrayal, like his, consisted in an inability to believe. Without faith she is incapable of passion, thence of love, finally of life itself.
>
> This is the "moral" of the story, translated as it is into the language of Christian theology: "Man cannot live by bread alone." Distilled even beyond that, into the language of statement, we might say that the theme is this: "Man cannot live if he accepts only materialistic values"; or, to put it into a positive statement: "Only in faith and love can man live." This does not, however, represent the "meaning," for the meaning is, as we have said, the total embodiment—the form. The statement is only an inadequate attempt on the part of the reader to seek out the author's intention. The question the student should ask next is, "How much does it leave unsaid?"

It is a little like shoveling sand in a windstorm to so much as begin to take issue with this crowd of New Critical pieties: the historical Christian assumptions as the ground for reading a "moral" statement; the fudging of the question of meaning by equating it simply with "form"; and the raising of the old specter of "intention." Miss Porter makes it quite clear that her intention is to elucidate the "desperate complications of her [the protagonist's] mind" and that the "meaning" of the story is in whatever general human nature can be discerned from such an elucidation. The "symbolic truth" Miss Porter speaks of is precisely in the way Laura's career corresponds to the ambiguous and paradoxical condition of recognizable modern man. Laura "is not at home in the world." In this configuration the most crucial fictional device is not the Judas tree but Laura herself. The theme, then, can hardly be stated as "man cannot live if he accepts only materialistic values." "Flowering Judas" dramatizes nothing so much as the fact that modern man, especially modern political man (Braggioni), lives and thrives, but more like a pig than a human. As for Laura, who has been enlisted in Braggioni's cause, she is so far from being materialistic that, in her "notorious virginity," she has even disowned her body. She is the most spiritual of women, but her spirit has been given over to a crusade founded not on a faith in the soul of man or the love of God but on the mindless force of history. In surrendering herself thus, she has surrendered everything.

If one must state a theme, it would be that of *self*-betrayal, and, more interestingly for a fictional construct, the way in which anomic modern life can be made of it.

> But she cannot help feeling that she has been betrayed irreparably by the disunion between her way of living and her feeling of what life should be, and at times she is almost contented to rest in this sense of grievance as a private store of consolation. Sometimes she wishes to run away, but she stays.

In their haste to see the meaning of "Flowering Judas" as inhering in its "most important" symbol, as it "occurs," commentators after the New Critics have failed consistently to distinguish the foreground of the narration from its shadowy, memorial background, where a series of rather theoretical and underdramatized "betrayed" characters have compromised Laura's Mexican life. Even Braggioni, despite his imminence and despite his taking part in the most affecting of scenes (his homecoming), curiously resides as almost exclusively an evil presence in Laura's desolate consciousness. There is, in fact, only one character upstage, Miss Porter's thrillingly intelligent narrative voice, guiding us over the landscape of Laura's mind, making sense for us of its "disunion." This she does in the historical present, so that the truth may be held up for inspection in life's continual moment.

CONSTANCE ROOKE and BRUCE WALLIS

Myth and Epiphany in Porter's "The Grave"

About a decade ago, there arose a flurry of critical interest in Katherine Anne Porter's story "The Grave." This inquiry quickly subsided, apparently satisfied that "The Grave" had been adequately explained. In fact it had not, for an intense preoccupation with the predominating symbols of the short story had entailed a concomitant limiting of critical focus, so that the widest implications of the story were ignored. In addition, the last note to emerge (some five years after the initial show of interest) pursued the tendency of the criticism which had preceded it to an impossible conclusion: the story was said to end with Miranda's re-repression of an unpleasant experience within the burial place of her mind. Focusing upon the few most obtrusive symbols—the ring, the dove, the rabbits, and the grave—criticism has continued to neglect the story's paradigm of our most primal racial myth, that of the fall of man, which is itself the pattern of a primal experience in the life of each individual.

The opening paragraph of the story, outlining the history of the family and its cemetery, immediately draws our attention to the continuing cycles of life and death, and to the journeys of mankind both in life and potentially beyond it. The reference to grandparents, establishing the existence of children and grandchildren, evokes the cycle of generations. In close conjunction with this, the removal from place to place of the grandmother, as well as of the "oddments of relations," and the grand-

From *Studies in Short Fiction* 3, vol. 15 (Summer 1978). Copyright © 1978 by Newberry College.

mother's repeated transportation of the grandfather's corpse ("as if she had set out to find her own burial place, knowing well she would never return to the places she had left") inevitably suggest the wandering movements of mankind on his larger journey through life toward death. The mention of eternity in the final sentence of the paragraph leaves latent the suggestion of a conclusion to the journey that carries beyond death.

In the following paragraph, the cemetery itself is more particularly described as a "pleasant small neglected garden of tangled rose bushes and ragged cedar trees and cypress, the simple flat stones rising out of uncropped sweet-smelling wild grass." It is, of course, difficult to encounter gardens in the work of any writer with a Catholic background without wondering if echoes of Eden are intended, but when the garden contains cedar and cypress trees—certainly existent in Texas, but most commonly associated with the Middle-East—our suspicions increase. Since in addition the garden is "neglected," the rose bushes are "tangled," and the cedar trees are "ragged," we may well begin to suppose of this garden which became a cemetery that it represents a fallen Eden.

Into the garden come Miranda and Paul. "Miranda," a name employed by Porter in a series of stories, obviously recalls the Miranda of Shakespeare's *The Tempest*, which made the name almost a synonym for innocence; John Fowles uses it with similar implications in *The Collector*. "Paul" might call to mind Paul the Apostle, except that it is as yet too early in the story to be certain of his function. At least we know that he is twelve, the conventional age of masculine puberty, the age at which Christ went to teach the elders in the temple. Miranda, at nine, would just be approaching this period of knowledge. This appearance in the garden of a male child and a female of slightly lesser age might also suggest Adam and Eve in a recapitulation of the childhood of our race.

The grave pits in this garden-cemetery are "all shaped alike with such purposeful accuracy" that the children dissemble awe as an appropriate response; yet the personal application of the message that death awaits all human beings has in fact eluded them. The same point is made when Miranda leaps "into the pit" that has "held her grandfather's bones," and, "scratching around aimlessly and pleasurably as any young animal," scoops up "a lump of earth" from the grave. A more chilling and a more tellingly compressed portrait of utter innocence in the face of death could scarcely be produced than appears in that eager leap into the grave of her own grandfather and in that equally oblivious weighing of a palmful of "pleasantly sweet, corrupt" smelling earth. But in the very rotting earth that summons up our mortal clay, Miranda also finds the dove, symbol (as several commentators have observed) of innocence and of the Holy

Ghost. Even before Miranda has fallen, and before death has become a reality to her, she discovers a token of her redemption.

At this point, significantly, she does not prize the dove. Trading it to Paul for the wedding ring (a specifically Freudian symbol of marriage and sex) which he has retrieved from another grave, she is clearly trading her innocence—so far through symbols only—for knowledge of the world and of her function as a woman. The suggestion of fertility in the "intricate flowers and leaves" carved on the ring adumbrates her awakening to this function, which at first takes the form of an interest in female luxury, but which occurs in earnest simultaneously with an awakening to sin and death when Miranda is confronted by the unborn baby rabbits. The ritual exchange, in which each child acquires the desired and appropriate token, is further marked by covetousness on each side. Miranda is "smitten at sight of the ring and wished to have it"; she glances "without covetousness," however, at the token which Paul, when "he had got the dove in his hand," identifies triumphantly as a " 'screw head for a *coffin!*' " Miranda's attraction to the ring seems perfectly natural, for "it fitted perfectly," but the implication is also that Miranda has yielded to an astutely calculated temptation. Satan, we remember, had relied upon Eve's vanity, and Porter will go on to develop this quality in Miranda. Paul's temptation seems directed toward his role as hunter. His interest in the dove is not yet as a token of immortality, but of death; it is important, therefore, that Paul has been identified as a hunter of doves and that in the breast of this dove there is a "deep round hollow" such as a bullet would make. He is aware, of course, that by means of this aperture the dove is affixed to the coffin, but he does not reflect that the function of this dove is to convey the spirit to its eternal home. Paul's attitude to his new possession exceeds the merely proprietorial: " 'I'll bet nobody else in the world has one like this!' " The desire for supremacy, which was to be derived from the knowledge of good and evil, which brought death into the world, and which would issue shortly in a particularly heinous murder (of Abel, or of the pregnant rabbit), is also a mark of the Fall.

Immediately following their appropriation of the ring and the dove, the children begin to feel uneasy: " 'Maybe we ought to go now,' she said, 'maybe one of the niggers'll see us and tell somebody.' " The change in their condition is signalled by the arrival of self-consciousness, by the fear of being observed and reported, and by the sense of having done something forbidden. As Adam and Eve were expelled from Eden, so Paul and Miranda feel "like trespassers" and know that they must leave the garden which is "no longer theirs." They take up their rifles and go off to hunt, much as our first parents were obliged to do. Informing us next that

"Miranda always followed at Paul's heels along the path, obeying instruc-
tions," Porter recalls the order of departure from Eden. "Unto the woman
he said, I will greatly multiply thy sorrow and thy conception; in sorrow
thou shalt bring forth children; and thy desire shall be to thy husband,
and he shall rule over thee" (*Genesis* 3:16). Miranda has yet to learn of
woman's special penalty in childbirth, but it is apparent that she knows
already something of the authority of man.

Porter chooses this moment to define for us the difference in
Miranda's and Paul's attitudes to hunting. Paul knows what he is doing
when he kills; he knows the act from intention to consequence, and is
already a small master in the world of experience. He is leader and teacher
not only because he is male and Miranda is female, but also because he is
older and more experienced than she. The realm into which Paul has
fallen is marked by the fact of death—and more, by the fact of killing; it is
a world in which actions have consequence, in which over and over again
the apple is eaten and the eater is punished. Miranda, on the other hand,
cares nothing about hitting the mark and is unaware of the consequences
of shooting beyond the immediate sensory experience of " 'pulling the
trigger and hearing the noise.' " That is, she is innocent. Still the
inhabitant of a floating Eden in which life is marvelous and without
consequence, Miranda crosses over only when she has seen the rabbits.
This apparent confusion about the moment of the Fall—for we have, after
all, just witnessed one representation of it, and yet are invited to believe
that Paul had fallen before this and Miranda only afterwards—is crucial to
the story's design, according to which everything happens both repeti-
tively and progressively, and in which events are returned to again and
again until their proper meaning has finally been understood.

That the Fall has in some sense not yet occurred for Miranda is
further indicated by her asking, on the way to the kill of the rabbit, if she
can " 'have the first snake.' " The reference here to the serpent in the
Garden of Eden is especially pointed because we have been specifically
told that Miranda and Paul regularly hunt rabbits and doves, not snakes.
No further mention of snakes is made, and this one reference is so clearly
artificially obtruded into a surface context to which it does not belong
that the author must carefully inform us that Miranda asks her question
"idly." If there has been any doubt that the story is concerned with the
myth of the Fall, such a conclusion now seems unavoidable.

Miranda asks her question about the snake "idly" also because her
interest in the hunt is slackening; it was never great, but now the ring is
glittering and directing her imagination elsewhere. Before Miranda's ring-
induced fantasies of adult womanhood are described, however, the author

supplies a digression concerned largely with the progress of sexual differentiation. In the course of this, Porter keeps us mindful of the Fall by references to sin and Scripture and by informing us that "the motherless family was running down" in part because Miranda's father (and so the children themselves) had been disinherited or "discriminated against" by the grandmother's will. The suggestions here of matriarchy—nearly of a female God—seem related in a compensatory fashion to the insistence (interesting in a woman writer) that before the Fall there was no difference between male and female. A curious and tattered remnant of unisexuality is contained in the "old women of the kind who smoke corn-cob pipes," who vociferously admire the departed matriarch of Miranda's family, and yet who criticize Miranda for wearing pants. Miranda's father is responsible for this aberration in the attire of his daughter; women such as those who chide Miranda, as the world progressed or fell, themselves took on the burden of policing the decorum of their sex. That Miranda still wears the same clothing as her brother is of course a reflection of her as yet unfallen state; although change is imminent, it seems "simple and natural" to her that she should dress in this way. The progress of female indoctrination is evidenced also in the case of Miranda's older sister, "the really independent and fearless one, in spite of her rather affected ways," who rides bareback and recklessly about the countryside. Maria's "affected ways" are the function of a proud, adolescent assumption of her role as lady; because she is "the really independent and fearless one," we are led to acknowledge the power of sexual convention which has begun to operate against her individual disposition and which will have sway also over Miranda.

The authorial insistence upon a gradually developed consciousness (whose movements seem fitful, unsynchronized, or repetitive) is apparent both in the incomplete sexualization of the two sisters and in Miranda's ability to accept (without laboring to reconcile) conflicting data from the world around her. On the one hand, Miranda's "powerful social sense" causes her to regret the dismay of the crones; and, on the other hand, she feels convinced by her father's arguments concerning the suitability of her attire. If the world of experience is chaotic, it does not appear so in a disturbing way to a child of Miranda's age. Similarly, she knows things without knowing how she knows, yet at this stage experiences no itch toward clarification. To establish this complexity of very gradual development—in the consciousness specifically of girls, more generally of children, and finally of human beings at any age—is a basic purpose of the digression. Such complexity, furthermore, is notably congruent with the authorial wheels-within-wheels strategy whereby the history of the race is recapitulated in the history of the individual.

The digression complete, Miranda sees the ring "shining with the serene purity of fine gold on her rather grubby thumb," and her feelings are directed "against her overalls and sockless feet." In imagination, she turns from Paul to Maria as her model. She wants to abandon the hunt, to return to the house, and to "dust herself with plenty of Maria's violet talcum powder . . . put on the thinnest, most becoming dress she owned, with a big sash, and sit in a wicker chair under the trees." This fantasy obviously works to prepare us for Miranda's acceptance of her destiny as woman, but it is also reminiscent of the Fall. As she was covetous of the ring, so now under its spell she experiences in the background of her apparently modest fantasy "vague stirrings of desire for luxury and a grand way of living which could not take precise form in her imagination but were founded on family legend of past wealth and leisure." Racial memory, the idea of a golden past belonging not only to the history of the family but also to the history of the race, is hinted at by the imprecision of Miranda's imaginings. In support of such an equation, we have carefully been informed that "leisure" is no longer the privilege of Miranda's family and that "she had been brought up in rigorous economy." The peculiarity here is that Miranda's "vague stirrings of desire" work backwards and forwards, attaching both to the past and to her desired future as a lady. She yearns for a prelapsarian state, when as a sort of queen she might sit "under the trees" of Eden, yet her "desires" are of dominion, restless, and directed toward the future so that simultaneously they express Eve's fall through vanity.

Miranda's fantasy is dispelled when Paul shoots the rabbit, and briefly she returns to a child's pleasure in the immediate, amoral moment. An echo of her fantasy, however, is contained in the information that "Uncle Jimbilly knew how to prepare the skins so that Miranda always had fur coats for her dolls, for though she never cared much for her dolls she liked seeing them in fur coats." Clearly, Miranda's present attraction to the idea of womanhood concerns the luxury rather than the maternity which may await her. Since everything happens by accretion in Porter's story, moreover, the ring has represented only a leap forward and not a beginning in Miranda's consciousness of herself as female.

Miranda's consciousness takes another, giant step forward when the children discover in the womb of the dead animal "a bundle of tiny rabbits." This is a brilliantly compressed image, functioning like Yeats's "dying generations" to express at once the brevity of life and the irony that all our growth (beginning with the moment of conception) is a

decline which culminates in death. Seeing these creatures whose tenure
upon earth has been so dramatically foreshortened, Miranda loses her
innocence in fact rather than in symbol. Whereas previously she had been
untroubled by the gradual accumulation of knowledge, now Miranda is
trembling at the brink of some absolute attainment: "she wanted most
deeply to see and to know. Having seen, she felt at once as if she had
known all along. The very memory of her former ignorance faded, she had
always known just this." Miranda has now assumed the knowledge of good
and evil; thus, she will reject the rabbit's skin. Additionally, she has taken
on the knowledge of life, birth, and death as they relate specifically to
herself as sinner, as woman, and as mortal being. In other words, in the
analogy she perceives between human babies (such as she has been and
will bear) and the dead-unborn baby rabbits covered with blood, she
recognizes her own mortality in all of its key aspects. Miranda's cavorting
in the grave like "any young animal" has acquired a new resonance.

The discovery of the baby rabbits is also significant to Paul, though
he speaks "as if he had known about everything all along." His particular
concern is that Miranda, toward whom his attitude is now conspiratorial,
should not cause punishment to descend upon him by revealing to their
father her loss of innocence. Similarly, he attempts concealment of his sin
when he hides the rabbits. The suggestion is that Paul, although his fall
has anticipated Miranda's, has nevertheless persisted in the hope of concealment entertained by Adam, and that he is as yet ignorant of Christ's
love as the only means of appeasing God's wrath.

Miranda represses the memory of the incident in the grave of her
mind, as the commentators also have pointed out, only to have it resurrected by the circumstances of the Mexican marketplace. The analogy to
her grandmother's transportation of her grandfather's corpse is clear. She
has herself moved on through the journey of life toward death: she is now
twenty-nine, and, "picking her path among the puddles and crushed
refuse of a market street in a strange city of a strange country," she is
obviously in exile. All the horror of her own mortality is suddenly
returned to Miranda by the raw "flesh," the wilting, funereal flowers, and
the "dyed sugar sweets, in the shapes of all kinds of small creatures"
—including "baby rabbits." But the "dreadful vision" fades when she
recalls her brother, "standing again in the blazing sunshine, again twelve
years old, a pleased sober smile in his eyes, turning the silver dove over
and over in his hands."

Clearly this vision of the dove is not a repression of the experience
with the rabbits, not a retreat into the easier memory of that day, but an
awakening to further knowledge. The "blazing sunshine" strongly suggests

revelation. The apostle Paul was on the road to Damascus—Miranda is also on a "path"—when "suddenly there shined round about him a light from heaven" (Acts 9:3), and he learned exactly what Miranda is shown learning here from the analogous vision of her own brother Paul. Though he was sin-ridden and ignorant of his potential salvation, precisely like Saul of Tarsus, there had come a time both for Paul and for his sister when the final lesson of that Texas day was understood. And it is entirely fitting, in the context of this miniature myth of the Fall, that the dove should have come out of the grave itself. It was, after all, the loss of innocence and the assumption of knowledge in the Garden of Eden, bringing death into life, that made the dove and what it represents both necessary and possible. Without the Fall and death, there would be no need for redemption and resurrection. So the dove, with its carefully mentioned screw-whorls, implying still another continuing cycle in a dynamically compressed image, suggests at once the brevity of death and the inevitability of new life. With its end in the "blazing sunshine" of such new knowledge, this is decidedly not the story of a willful self-blinding, but rather of an epiphany of the first water.

JOAN GIVNER

Katherine Anne Porter, Journalist

When she read in a psychology text-
book that childhood experiences reconstructed are sometimes entirely
true, sometimes undeniably false, and mostly a mixture of truth and
falsehood, Katherine Anne Porter (who habitually read with pencil in
hand) wrote in the margin that the cure for this unhappy state of affairs
was to become an honest writer of fiction. Becoming a writer, however,
did not entirely cure her tendency to shape and order the events of her
own life as if she were writing a story and holding taut the thread of her
theme. She heightened those events which she thought important and
completely suppressed others which she thought did not really belong to
her and should never have happened. One area of experience which she
rejected was her work as a journalist. Since she decided that it had no
bearing on her growth as an artist she forgot that she did newspaper work
for long and that she ever took it seriously. Her attitude is summed up in
these words:

> I forgive that critic here and now, and forever, for calling me a "newspaper
> woman" in the public prints. I consider it actionable libel, but, as is too
> often the case in these incidents, he has a small patch of solid ground
> under him. . . .
> Fifty-odd years ago, for eight short months of my ever-lengthening
> (or shortening?) life, I did have a kind of a job on a newspaper, *The
> Rocky Mountain News*.

Such statements are unfortunate because they have deflected attention
from material which is crucial to the understanding of Porter's life and art.

From *Southwest Review* 4, vol. 64 (Autumn 1979). Copyright © 1979 by Southern Methodist
University.

On September 15, 1917, just one year before she started work on the *Rocky Mountain News*, Katherine Anne Porter was introduced to readers of Fort Worth's *The Critic* as "coming from the staff of several prominent newspapers" to devote her young life to their paper. For several months she wrote up society notes and theatrical performances for *The Critic*, and her work is entirely appropriate to one described in the paper as "liking things which other people consider frivolous and of no consequence." Any play or musical which showed "Cupid's career from beginning to end" was likely to be treated with indulgent amusement.

Fort Worth at the time was badly in need of light entertainment. The city was a ferment of military activity with thousands of soldiers stationed on the outskirts, being trained for service in Europe. As the fall turned to winter the weather became cold and rainy and many of the soldiers fell ill with stomach ailments, pneumonia, and contagious diseases. The military hospitals were inadequate for such emergencies and many of the sick soldiers were housed in makeshift tents in cold, miserable conditions. The people of Fort Worth rallied to help, and the young women of the Red Cross Corps were foremost among the volunteers. Porter joined the Corps and was immediately given the job of publicity chairman. She threw herself wholeheartedly into the job and wrote for the newspaper many articles describing and promoting the work of the Red Cross Corps.

The articles she wrote have the interest of describing events which she also used in her story "Pale Horse, Pale Rider." The comparison of factual accounts of Porter's experiences with their fictional version is always instructive, providing as it does another illustration of her remark that her fiction is really reportage, that she arranges it and it is fiction but that it really happened. The comparison of the Fort Worth newspaper articles with the version of the events in the story show a complete reversal in her attitude to the experiences. In the newspaper she is full of admiration for the work of the society girls who have abandoned pleasure for the rigors of Red Cross service:

> . . . . they are discovering a bit earlier than their predecessors that which all of us discover soon or late—that life is a long process of riddance in which we slowly strip our souls of superficialities and find that we have left at last only a few big universal things that really count. Even three years ago what society girls studied the problems of immigration or pure food, or tenements or clean milk for poor little neglected babies? Which one of them dreamed of giving a fixed portion of her time to a certain work, reporting at headquarters and taking her orders like a little soldier? Yet here they are deep in war work doing their bit coura-

geously. As one of them said only yesterday, "It is bigger than I am, all this. But I couldn't let go now. I don't know how I used to fill my days! And even when the war is over I don't think we can ever go back to living entirely for ourselves alone. Wouldn't it be dull and empty?" And wouldn't it though?

In the weeks before Christmas she is enthusiastic in her support for the Social Service Club's Cheer Fund which worked to provide a pleasant Christmas for the soldiers at the Camp Bowie Base hospital:

> Dimes to dollars—every man, woman and chee-ild who passes just about any corner of the downtown district, will be offered a becoming red, blue and white tag. The money thus accumulated will be used for the Christmas goodies of the sick soldiers at Camp Bowie and they hope to have enough money to give every man in the hospital a present.
>
> Misses Beniti McElwee, Sophie Bahan, Irene Bryan and many others have it in charge and are prepared to place squads of cheer members right where they will do most good, with the firm intention of accepting anything from a dime to a dollar and above for each and every little taglet they attach to any button, collar, overcoat or fur muff whatsoever. So, do pray, stand very meekly to attention and render up your ill-gotten wealth, remembering you are but the outward symbol to these girls, leave spare something to tie a tag on, without regard to age, sex, creed or previous condition of servitude. Don't howl "Murder, murder," or anything of the sort as you do when you pay your church dues, but keep in mind your dime or dollar will make the holiday pleasant for the luckless sick on Christmas Day at Camp Bowie. Do your Christmas giving early—and cheerfully.

And she describes the appreciation of the girls' work by the soldiers in glowing terms:

> Accompanied by their chaperones—even in social service the conventions are in order—the committee makes weekly visits to the hospital with flowers, fruit, magazines and best of all from the soldier-boy point of view, home made cake for the sick and convalescent who are allowed to partake of such dainties. Hospital days are twice as long as ordinary ones and the presence of friendly faces and gay voices will help eke out the monotonous round of the clock.
>
> After only three visits the men have begun to look forward to Friday, dolling all up for the occasion and appearing nicely shaved and brushed and polite—The ones who are really sick—they have a good many of those now—complain and tell of their little-boy grievances and troubles, sure of sympathy and understanding and real interest. It's too bad so many of them had to go out and get measles and mumps and such like ailments of extreme youth.
>
> The girls are taking books out there now. One asked for poetry

and was delighted with a wee, white, pink-rosed gift book of Scott's "Lady of the Lake" which he vowed he would memorize.

When these events are transformed into fiction the attitude of the Red Cross Corps is depicted as grudging, cynical, and hostile. One of them says of entertaining the soldiers:

> . . . .we must do everything we can to make them feel contented, but I draw the line at talking to them. I told the chaperones at those dances for enlisted men, I'll dance with them, every dumbell who asks me, but I will NOT talk to them, I said, even if there is a war. So I danced hundreds of miles without opening my mouth except to say Please keep your knees to yourself.

Miranda Gay, the main character in the story, is one of their number, and she is miserably embarrassed by the idiocy of the work. The whole business is seen as an exercise in futility, and the recipients of the charity are as jaundiced as those who perform it:

> Miranda, with her wilting bouquet and her basket of sweets and ciga-rettes, looking about, caught the unfriendly bitter eye of a young fellow lying on his back, his right leg in a cast and pulley. She stopped at the foot of his bed and continued to look at him, and he looked back with an unchanged hostile face. Not having any, thank you and be damned to the whole business, his eyes said plainly to her, and will you be so good as to take your trash off my bed?

Neither the cause nor the date of this about-face is obscure, for Porter has described in detail the events of this period of her life. In the fall of 1918 she had been working for just one month on the *Rocky Mountain News* when she fell ill with the plague of influenza which swept the United States in the last months of World War I. She was taken to a hospital and left behind screens to die. Her obituary was written up for the paper, and her family made the arrangements for her funeral. A group of young interns, however, decided to give her an experimental injection of strychnine, and she rallied and survived. When she emerged from the hospital her world was completely changed. She had lost all her hair, she had a broken elbow because she had been made to walk too soon, and she had phlebitis in her left leg. The war was over and the young man who had nursed her before she was admitted to hospital had caught the plague and died. But the main change was in her mental state. She described it long afterward to an interviewer: "It just simply divided my life, cut across it like that. So that everything before was just getting ready. It took me a long time to go out and live in the world again. I was really alienated, in the pure sense."

In her fictional version of these events she also describes her main character, Miranda Gay, as being emotionally quite changed. She describes Miranda's hardened indifferent heart shuddering in despair at itself "because before it had been tender and capable of love."

The change of heart described in the interview and the story is reflected in the journalism which Porter wrote after she recovered. When she resumed work in February, 1919, she was dramatic editor of the *Rocky Mountain News* and in that capacity wrote many signed theatrical reviews and some editorials which are unsigned but unmistakably in her style. The tone and attitude are entirely different from those of the year before. The glib style and the embarrassing mannerisms have disappeared, and there is a new sureness in her style and a conviction in her opinion which mark these works as her first serious literary criticism.

Like much of the criticism which she wrote over her lifetime, it is frankly moralistic in tone. (One of her favorite remarks was Virginia Woolf's statement that the one advantage of having a settled mode of morals is that you know exactly what to laugh at.) In one review she gives a scathing account of a soldier's telling his war experiences in a half-empty hall, while people lined up on the other side of the street to see some scantily dressed dancing girls:

> An average audience faced the soldier who had lived thru the most profound experiences ever offered to humanity on this sad earth: and there they sat, looking calmly ahead, while the aviator told them a few unattractive truths about themselves, the Bolsheviki and kindred evils. When we came out of this theater, the crowd on the other side of the street had extended half way down the block on either side of the magic portals. All to glimpse six scampering· chorus girls inadequately clad! Forgive these slightly ironic smiles—it was amusing.
>
> A study of their faces under the sharp sidewalk lights revealed a really serious appreciation of art, so to speak. That is, they seriously wished to be present when the parade started. Some of them wedged in, and the disappointed ones were still there, augmented by several hundred additional devotees of the drama when the lucky ones wended forth late in the evening, wearing surfeited cat-and-cream smiles. There was nothing scandalous in the whole affair save the mental atmosphere. That was somewhat suffocating we admit.

By this time she has no illusions about the quality of the plays and no hesitation in voicing her scorn for them. When Cupid's career is gone over, her contempt is boundless and her only words of praise are for the actors. In a May 4 review of *The Woman on the Index* by George Broadhurst she describes the play as a "poor corpse" which a company of capable actors "galvanized into life with their pleasant personalities." In a number of reviews she scorns the inevitable happy ending, mocks the subject matter (love presented as "an ethereal affair ending sedately at the altar with an exchange of vows" and marriage as a "long roseate picnic"), and attacks the weak plots.

Nor does she single out individual plays alone for criticism; she condemns the whole of the drama of the day. She says in one review, answering those who bewail the deterioration of theatrical standards, that she doubts if the theater ever was the pillar of the fine arts. Rather she believes it has always been "cheap and callow or else bombastic and hideously untrue to life and art." In a review of *The Man Who Came Back* by J.E. Goodman she says categorically that she considers modern drama to be a "slander on life, on art, on—pardon the stodginess—on morals," and she rejects its facile optimism:

> Most of us care little for art, and are terrified of life. So, therefore, our moral truths must be doled out to us in sugar pills of sentimentality. We cannot endure to see people being punished for wrongdoing or dying in the last act. We must be cheered up and slapped on the back and assured that everything is for the best in this best of all possible worlds.

The following review presents her opinion of the drama in summary:

> Of plays and books, especially those of the current season there is not much to be said. Flaccid and flavorless most of them are; the plays have been a wearying procession of saccharine he-and-she affairs, with a coarseness that passes for comedy and a brutality that passes for strength. The plots creak in both books and plays, the long arm of coincidence is being fairly snatched from the socket half the time.

It is apparent from Porter's descriptions of the simpering heroines and stereotypical heroes and villains that the theatrical fare of the time consisted mainly of crude Victorian melodrama. But what is interesting is that while she objects strenuously to the plays she does not question or reject the basic characteristics of melodrama itself. The form, in fact, is completely acceptable to her. She accepts, for example, the polarization of good and evil and the division of characters into saints and sinners. In an untitled editorial on the villains of stage and screen she mocks the exaggerated, unconvincing, stereotypical appearance of the usual villain, but she does not question the existence of the villain himself:

> Screen villains are for the most part basely [sic] untrue to life. They have no respect for the police and very little for the neighbors. They make scenes in hotel lobbies which is in very bad taste and always openly persecute the heroine, which is bad judgment. . . .

> The screen villain's clothes are usually all wrong and his moustache deceives no one. Yet he is not without interest in many respects, tho' after attending a series of pictures we have an uncanny feeling that we are meeting the same man again and again in varying disguises.

She goes on, having dubbed him "Everyvillain," to trace his trail of crime in his various manifestations as a tall, dark, moustached man, as a blond balding type in a business suit, as a middle-aged impresario, and as an aesthete. Her descriptions are readable and amusing, and they show that she objects not to the concept of the villain but to the quality of the villains being presented.

In the same review, one of the most revealing of her attitudes, she says that she has had a "longstanding fascination with the psychology of villainy." She then modifies her statement, explaining that the real villain deserves some admiration because, after all, "it takes imagination and real nerve to become a real first class sinner." In another review she expresses the opinion that a sinner is more interesting than a saint probably because "he is often a trifle more sincere."

Since she recognized the positive qualities to be found in the villain, she transferred her attention from the villain to the virtuous, passive heroine, and it was on this figure that she eventually focused all her scorn and contempt. She felt that the attempt to pass off such a feeble person as the receptacle of virtue was not only bad art, but also, in her own phrase, a "slander on morals." Many reviews, like the following one of George Broadhurst's *The Woman on the Index*, express her impatience:

> It must be true that Broadhurst wrote the role of Sylvia Angot, the heroine—the deadly virtuous deeply wronged creature who spends a great deal of valuable time concealing her past from her highly respected husband. None but a Broadway playwright could cast such a sickly halo around the head of a straw woman. "Look," says he, "look, how this saintly woman is being wronged by everybody in sight, and see how pure she is. Look at this husband who must never, never know or he would turn from her in horror."
> And he proceeds to build up a tissue of bogus, near crimes, wherein he tangles the lady, and sets her to work concealing a past that she wouldn't need to conceal if she had a grain of intelligence. But, of course, she hasn't or she wouldn't be the heroine of a Broadway drama.

The shift of Porter's attention from the villain to the saintly heroine was not a temporary change of focus but a permanent one, and her attitude toward the virtuous heroine eventually formed the cornerstone of her moral philosophy. The main tenet of this philosophy is that the evildoers are not the most reprehensible people in the world, because they at least have the courage of their convictions. Nor are they the most dangerous people, since they can be easily recognized. The people who really need to be watched are the so-called innocents who stand by and allow others to perpetrate evil. Porter was to express repeatedly the opinion that the innocent bystanders allow the activity of evildoers, not merely because of fear and indifference, but because they gain vicarious pleasure from seeing others perform the wicked deeds which they themselves wish but fear to perform. She came eventually to see the passive virtuous people as guilty of promoting evil even when they do not consciously to do so.

This theory about the relationship between saints and evildoers and their collusion in evil became her lifelong gospel, the subject of numerous informal talks, the message she preached from political platforms, and the basis of her interpretation of current events. After the publication of *Ship of Fools* she gave this account of some of the events of the twentieth century:

> . . . . the collusion in evil that allows creatures like Mussolini, or Hitler, or Huey Long or McCarthy—you can make your own list, petty and great—to gain hold of things, who permits it? Oh, we're convinced we're not evil. We don't believe in that sort of thing, do we? And the strange thing is that if these agents of evil are all clowns, why do we put up with them? God knows, such men are evil, without sense—forces of pure ambition and will—but they enjoy our tacit consent.

Her judgments in literary criticism were influenced by the same point of view. She praised Eudora Welty's stories because she depicted villains pure and unmitigated and with none of the sympathy and understanding which Porter believed amounted to criminal collusion in evil between author and character. Consistently, when Robert Penn Warren published *All the King's Men* she wrote to various friends of her shock and horror that he should have explored carefully the motivation of the character based on Huey Long. She felt that he should have portrayed the character as a villain, and she condemned the book as a sentimental apology for the worst kind of fascist demogogue.

The same theory informed all her fiction. An early spare version of her theme appears in the short story "Magic." Here a maid, hoping to relax her mistress as she brushes her hair, tells a story of a villainous madam who cheats and bullies the prostitutes in a New Orleans brothel. The point of the story is that the madam's activity is made possible by those around her—the male clients, the police, and the cook—who do nothing. Not only are these people as guilty as the one who perpetrates the violence, but so too are the woman and the maid who relish the story. The woman sniffs scent (a detail which suggests her desire to hide the unpleasant realities), stares at her blameless reflection in the mirror, and urges the storyteller to continue whenever she pauses. Lest there be any doubt about the equation of guilt between both madams and both maids, they resemble each other so closely as to invite confusion. When the storyteller describes the cook of the brothel she might be describing herself: "she was a woman, colored like myself with much French blood all the same, like myself always among people who worked spells. But she had a very hard heart, she helped the madam in everything, she liked to watch all that happen." The theme of the story echoes Porter's words that the evil of our time is not an accident but a total consent.

A fuller version of the theme appears in "Flowering Judas," which, like many of Porter's stories, has a triangular arrangement of characters, consisting of villain, victim, and "heroine." Braggioni, like all Porter's villains, is pure caricature and looms in the story like a grotesque Easter egg in shades of mauve and purple and yellow. A hideous creature with the eyes of a cat and the paunch of a pig, he embodies each of the seven deadly sins.

The implication of the story is that if Braggioni is a self-serving, self-indulgent villain, he has not always been so. Once he was a young idealist in both politics and love. It is Laura and people like her who have caused him to change from idealist to opportunist, and the main focus of the story is upon her and upon her motivation. She neither loves nor opposes Braggioni, because she is basically indifferent to him as she is to most people. She has trained herself to remain uncommitted in her relationships with others and has developed a principle of rejection: ". . . . the very cells of her flesh reject knowledge and kinship in one monotonous word. No. No. No. She draws her strength from this one holy talismanic word which does not suffer her to be led into evil. Denying everything she may walk anywhere in safety, she looks at everything without amazement." It is the death of Eugenio in which she has conspired with Braggioni that causes her finally to become aware of her guilt, and then only in a dream. As she falls asleep she receives a message from her own depths which warns her of motives and the meaning of her acts.

Porter's longest treatment of her theme is, of course, *Ship of Fools*. She described her intentions in the novel in a 1946 letter to Josephine Herbst. She said that her book was about the constant endless collusion between good and evil. She said that she believed human beings to be capable of total evil but thought that no one had ever been totally good, and that gave the edge to evil. She intended not to present any solution, but simply to show the principle at work and why none of us had an alibi in the world. She said that her plan and conclusion had been worked out ten years before and that nothing had happened since to change her mind—indeed, everything confirmed her old opinion.

Again in the novel the villains are depicted in caricature. Herr Rieber is piglike and the Zarzuela Company, a group of thieves, pimps, and prostitutes who stop at nothing, is described as a flock of crows or other quarreling, thieving birds.

The pivotal character who corresponds with Laura of "Flowering Judas" is Dr. Schumann. He is well qualified by his superior intelligence and by his professional training to be influential, but he has developed a detachment which distances him from the others. He is introduced in the novel standing above the other characters to watch them come aboard. As he looks down from his elevated position his interest is clinical, aloof. The hunchback stirs his interest as a case of extreme malformation; Jenny excites his disapproval as an immodest woman; and Mrs. Treadwell with her bruise arouses his worst, and as it turns out, totally unfounded suspicions. Typically, he soon loses interest, and it is apparent that his physical weakness of the heart is symptomatic of a corresponding spiritual weakness. He is a professional helper of mankind who gives help automatically but is incapable of love or involvement. When the Captain asks his advice on what to do about the Zarzuela Company his reply, "Do nothing at all," marks his kinship with Laura. Like her, he eventually experiences a moment when the implications of his acts become apparent, even to himself: "The Doctor suffered the psychic equivalent of a lightning stroke, which cleared away there and then his emotional fogs and vapors, and he faced his truth, nearly intolerable but the kind of pain he could deal with, something he recognized and accepted unconditionally."

Within the novel the theme is stated in a crucial discussion which takes place at the Captain's table of the *Vera*. The guests are discussing the activities of the Spanish dancers, and Frau Rittersdorf expresses the opinion that they are "dangerous criminals." The Captain disagrees because "it requires a certain force of character to be really evil." (His remark has the special interest of being almost word for word what Katherine Anne Porter wrote in 1919 in her editorial on the villains of the Denver stage.) Dr. Schumann elaborates on the Captain's statement:

> I agree with the Captain it takes a strong character to be really evil.
> Most of us are too slack, half-hearted or cowardly—luckily, I suppose.

Our collusion with evil is only negative, consent by default you might say. I suppose in our hearts our sympathies are with the criminal because he really commits the deed we only dream of doing.

Katherine Anne Porter was not embarrassed by her changelessness and indeed often congratulated herself on it. After the publication of her novel she said: "It's astonishing how little I've changed: nothing in my point of view or way of feeling. I'm going back now to finish some of the great many short stories that I have begun and not been able to finish for one reason or another."

In the last years of her life she did complete a number of stories and essays which she had started earlier, among them an account of her participation in the movement protesting the execution of Sacco and Vanzetti in Boston in 1927. Her publication of her essay, *The Never Ending Wrong*, fifty years later made it the work with the longest gestation period, twenty years longer than that of *Ship of Fools*.

Reactions to the book were mixed. Others who were involved in the Sacco-Vanzetti case felt that the writers who flocked to Boston did so seeking grist for conversations in such gathering places of the literati as the round table of the Algonquin. One reviewer felt that the essay was an inconsequential work which told too little about the case and too much about how Porter felt on every occasion of human betrayal. Only Porter's friend Eudora Welty pointed out the close thematic link between the essay and the fiction. In fact, the theme of the essay is exactly that of the stories and the novel, the arrangement of characters in a triangle of villain, victim, and not-so-innocent hero/heroine, the same that appears in all her work.

The villains have all the recognizable porcine, complacent traits of such other villains as Braggioni and Herr Rieber. They are Governor Fuller, Judge Thayer (who is reported to have said while playing golf, "Did you see what I did to those anarchistic bastards?"), and the Judges who preside over the trial of the picketers and who are described as follows:

> . . . . three entirely correct old gentleman looking much alike in their sleekness, pinkness, baldness, glossiness of grooming, such stereotypes as no proletarian novelist would have dared to use as the example of a capitalist monster in his novel. . . . The gentlemen regarded us glossily, then turned to each other. As we descended the many floors in silence, one of them said to the others in a cream-cheese voice, "It is very pleasant to know that we may expect things to settle down properly again," and the others nodded with wise, smug, complacent faces.

Arrayed against these representatives of corrupt authority are all those who wish to help the victims and protest their unfair trial. On close inspection, however, they turn out like other of Porter's blameless people to be secretly in collusion with the villains and conspiring toward the same end. Chief among these are the Communists, represented by Rosa Baron. When Porter expressed the wish that the victims might be saved, she was astonished to hear Rosa Baron reply, "Why, what on earth good would they be to us alive?" And there are other protesters of dubious intention, notably the journalists who profit from the scenes of high emotion when the members of the victim's family appear. One gloats that he arranged the whole show. The victims, of course, are not saved and they die, like Eugenio of "Flowering Judas" and Echegaray of *Ship of Fools*, with dignity and resignation gazing steadfastly at death. Their families are dazed and filled with horror, as are many of Porter's characters when they recognize the presence of Evil, "its power and its bestial imbecility."

Students of her work have assumed that Porter is another writer whose philosophy developed out of her reaction to the rise of Nazism. The assumption is a logical one, for she had more reason than most writers to be affected by that phenomenon, since she witnessed it at first hand. She spent several months in late 1931 and 1932 living in Berlin, and besides attending political rallies she made friends with at least one Nazi leader. And she has said that being on the German boat, S.S. *Werra*, from Vera Cruz to Bremerhaven in 1931 was a godsent experience for her as a writer. She had added that she would not have been able to place the German experience in perspective if she had not seen similar things happening earlier in Mexico.

The experiences in Mexico and Germany, however, did not produce new opinions so much as they confirmed and strengthened already existing ones. Porter's journalism shows that her lifelong philosophy was already shaped before she went to Mexico and that it developed out of her attempt to write criticism of her contemporary theater.

"One of the most disturbing tendencies of the human mind," Katherine Anne Porter wrote in 1936, "is its wilful and destructive forgetting of whatever in its past does not flatter or confirm its present point of view." Her own tendency to forget how long and how seriously she worked as a newspaperwoman has long obscured an important thematic principle in her work.

THOMAS F. WALSH

The Dreams Self in
"Pale Horse, Pale Rider"

Deriving its title from an old spiritual, Katherine Anne Porter's "Pale Horse, Pale Rider" tells how Death carries off Adam, "a sacrificial lamb" who is "committed without any knowledge or act of his own to death," leaving Miranda the "one singer to mourn." Therefore some critics have read the story as a tragedy of circumstances in which war and disease doom its star-crossed lovers. Wayne Booth writes that the reader is united with Miranda "against the hostile world around her" as she travels "alone toward the discovery that the man she loves has died." He also stresses her "moral superiority": "She must be accepted at her own estimate from the beginning," for "the slightest suggestion that she is at fault" or "that the author and reader are observing [her] from above rather than alongside will destroy, at least in part, the quality of our concern and hence of our final revelation." Yet, in the story's five dream (or delirium) sequences, we do observe Miranda "from above" without sacrificing our concern for her. They are the most subjective parts of "Pale Horse, Pale Rider" because they reveal the hidden undercurrents of her mind, but they are also the most objective because they enable the reader to understand her in a way that she never understands herself. Miranda's dreams offer convincing evidence that the agonizing circumstances of war and disease trigger rather than cause her despair at the end of the story, bringing to the surface what lay submerged in her character prior to their event. She seizes upon the circumstances but never completely grasps the underlying causes of her discontent.

From *Wascana Review* 2, vol. 14 (Fall 1979). Copyright © 1980 by *Wascana Review*.

Examining the story's five dreams in detail, I shall show that: the opening dream of the Pale Rider establishes the ironic pattern of the story and reveals early symptoms of Miranda's discontent that strongly resemble those of the ontologically insecure person of R.D. Laing's *The Divided Self*; Adam is a narcissistic projection of Miranda, this discussion relating to Laing's study and encompassing a reading of the second, third and fourth dreams; Miranda's long fifth dream dramatizes the crisis of her desperate physical and psychological struggle with life and death, resulting in her Pyrrhic victory over influenza and in her alienation from the world of the living; and Porter, like Miranda, came to consider her own near-death from influenza more significant to her than her love, her story indirectly serving as a justification of her conception of herself as artist.

The story's opening dream reveals Miranda's chronic inner struggle with life and death. She envisions herself in her childhood home, readying for a pre-dawn journey that she does not "mean to take": "Daylight will strike a sudden blow on the roof startling them all to their feet; faces will beam asking, Where are you going, What are you doing, What are you thinking, How do you feel, Why do you say such things, What do you mean? . . . How I have loved this house in the morning before we are all awake and tangled together like badly cast fishing lines. . . ." She wonders where "that lank greenish stranger" is, as if she were looking for him, and then decides to saddle her horse and outrun "Death and the Devil." The stranger then appears and rides with her, "regarding her without meaning, the blank still stare of mindless malice that makes no threats and can bide its time," but she tells him to ride on, after which she "slowly, unwillingly" awakens, waiting "in a daze for life to begin again." Then "a gong of warning" reminds her of the war which she had "happily" forgotten.

Not remembering her dream, Miranda thinks that sleep is a happy escape from the war: while bathing, she "wished she might fall asleep there, to wake up only when it was time to sleep again." Later in the day her desire to escape becomes an explicit death wish: "There's too much of everything in this world right now. I'd like to sit down here on the curb . . . and die, and never again see—I wish I could lose my memory and forget my own name. . . ." But her dream of the Pale Rider suggests that Miranda's fear and insecurity are rooted, not in the present circumstance of war, but in her childhood. The young Miranda awakes before her family to escape their demands which she considers a threat to the self; her escape is from the human condition, conceived in terms of sleepers who are shocked into an unhappy resurrection by the sun and become hopelessly entangled with each other as it runs its course until they can sleep and forget again. Her fluctuating attraction and aversion to the Pale

Rider reveal her paradoxical attempt through death to preserve the self from extinction by others and her determination to live on despite her fears. She rejects the Pale Rider and with him the dream-escape itself as she waits "in a daze for life to begin again," just as the sleepers in her dream would be "startled" to life by a "blow of daylight." The irony is that her forgotten dream of escaping the war has played out the hopelessness of her escaping anything, which she learns at the end of the story: having been shocked back to life on Armistice day, "she folded her painful body together and wept silently, shamelessly, in pity for herself and her lost rapture. There was no escape."

The opening dream is a paradigm of Miranda's unbearable dilemma throughout the story; fearing life and death, she reluctantly chooses life which she likens to death. Her condition is similar to that of Laing's ontologically insecure person who "may feel more unreal than real; in a literal sense, more dead than alive; precariously differentiated from the rest of the world, so that his identity and autonomy are always in question." Particularly relevant is the insecure person's feeling of "engulfment," in which he fears that he will lose his identity and autonomy in any relationship with another or "even with himself." "Engulfment is felt as a risk in being understood (thus grasped, comprehended), in being loved, or simply in being seen."

Miranda's flight from the well-meaning questions of her family is an explicit example of her fear of being understood. Just as she seeks sleep as an escape from war, a temporary death which preserves her life, so in the dream she wishes her family temporarily dead because awake they and she become "tangled together like badly cast fishing lines," an image of her fear of losing her autonomous identity. In an essay Porter quotes with approval Willa Cather's fear of the family: "Yet every individual in that household . . . is clinging passionately to his individual soul, is in terror of losing it in the general family flavor. . . . Always in his mind each member is escaping, running away, trying to break the net which circumstances and his own affections have woven about him."

The common ingredient in Miranda's dream and in Cather's passage is the fear of engulfment or entrapment, expressed by the fishing line and net images. Cather implies that this fear in some form is a common experience. Laing would agree, pointing out that in the "comprehensible transition" from the sane to the psychotic, "*sanity or psychosis is tested by the degree of conjunction or disjunction between two persons where one is sane by common consent.*" The key word is "degree." I find that the degree of Miranda's disjunction between herself and the world is remarkable enough to view her symptoms in light of Laing's study, but not as remarkable as, for example, Mr. Helton's disjunction in "Noon Wine," the second story of *Pale Horse, Pale Rider*; obviously Miranda is sane and Helton is not.

Another symptom of Miranda's engulfment is her dread of related-ness even with herself which she expresses in her uncertain response to the Pale Rider as Death and the Devil: "Ah, I have seen this fellow before, I know this man if I could place him. He is no stranger to me." Miranda confronts an aspect of herself which she fears and hates and for that reason is not quite able to recognize. The Pale Rider as Death symbolizes her deathwish. As the Devil he symbolizes her pervasive fear that she is evil to others as they are to her.

Miranda's sense of mutual danger and distrust between herself and others is reflected by the Pale Rider's "blank still stare of mindless malice" and by her preoccupation with eyes throughout the story. His stare is matched by the "really stony, really viciously cold" stare of the Liberty Bond salesman and by the "malign eyes" of the rainbow-colored birds of her second dream. The "unfriendly bitter" eyes of the hospitalized soldier anticipate Miranda's own "covertly hostile eyes of an alien" as she too lies in a hospital bed at the end of the story. Her eyes reveal her sense of betrayal, yet the hostility of all the eyes has a common source in her mind; without realizing it, the betrayed are self-betrayed. Her remark that "the worst of the war is the fear and suspicion and the awful expression in all the eyes you meet . . . as if they had pulled down the shutters over their minds and their hearts and were peering out at you, ready to leap if you make one gesture or say one word they do not understand instantly" applies equally to her. The "hard unblinking point of light" of her last dream represents her loveless determination to survive in a hostile world against which she has formed her defense. Laing notes that to the insecure individual "every pair of eyes is in a Medusa's head which he feels has power actually to kill or deaden something precariously vital to him. He tries therefore to forestall his own petrifaction by turning others to stone." Miranda's preoccupation with hostile eyes obviously does not assume such an extreme form although she notes the "really stony" stare of the bond salesman. Her hostile eyes, if they do not petrify others, serve defensively to counteract their hostility.

Miranda's dream and painful recollection of the preceding day are partially offset by her love for Adam, who "was in her mind so much, she hardly knew when she was thinking about him directly." Although the first fifteen pages of the story offer no evidence that he was in her mind, we still must question how Miranda in love is like the engulfed person who "regards his own love and that of others as being as destructive as hatred." One answer is that he longs for and needs love, but, as Laing points out, his longing and need are not enough to overcome his dread. This applies to Miranda, the poignancy of whose story does not lie only in Adam's death, but also in her belief that she could love him if he had lived.

One disturbing note in Miranda's love for Adam is the frequency with which she expresses her pessimism about their future together: ". . . he was not for her nor for any woman, being beyond experience already, committed without any knowledge or act of his own to death"; she "faced for one instant that was a lifetime the certain, the overwhelming and awful knowledge that there was nothing at all ahead for Adam and for her"; "Pure, she thought, all the way through, flawless, complete, as the sacrificial lamb must be." The uncertainties of wartime alone cannot account for Miranda's insistence on Adam's death; her frequent premonitions betray her unconscious desire that he die, for she fears love: " 'I don't want to love,' she would think in spite of herself, 'not Adam, there is no time and we are not ready for it and yet this is all we have—.' "

Miranda's ambivalent response to love also explains her idealization of Adam as pure and flawless, a prelapsarian Adam who cannot survive in the fallen world of war, disease, and human love. Her inclination to idealize him out of existence reveals not only her fear of accepting him as real, but also her idealization of herself. Adam does not seem real because he is a narcissistic projection of Miranda—that is, her double.

The clues to the doubling relation are that Miranda and Adam are "twenty-four years old each, alive and on the earth at the same moment," both are Texans, are vain about their appearance, indulging in the purchase of expensive clothes, keep "unwholesome" hours, and like to swim, dance and smoke. Like many doubles Adam almost seems a hallucination: he keeps company with Miranda in the late evening and is alone with her during the day, even in public places, talking exclusively to her except for a brief exchange with her landlady.

Miranda's vanity touches on the reasons for the doubling relation. Adam tells her, "I think you're beautiful" and when she later returns the compliment in almost exactly the same words, he objects to the inappropriate adjective, but the point is that she unconsciously applies it to herself, seeing her beauty in him. Significantly, the sentence telling us that Adam's "image was simply always present" in her thoughts is immediately followed by "She examined her face in the mirror. . . ."

Miranda's vanity is a manifestation of that narcissism which Otto Rank defines in its broadest sense as self-love in which is "rooted the instinct for self-preservation, and from which emerges the deep and powerful longing to escape death, or the submergence into nothingness, and the hope of awakening to a new life. . . ." In this sense all are narcissistic, but narcissism becomes extreme to the degree that a person, in his inordinate fear of aging and death, is unable to accept his own limitations in time. His consuming preoccupation with self prevents him from loving another. Desperately attempting to realize his ideal self, he may provoke the appearance of his double who represents that self or hated aspects of his personality which fall short of the ideal.

Miranda's narcissism in its purest form appears in her fifth dream as the "minute fiercely burning particle of being that knew itself alone, that relied upon nothing beyond itself for its strength . . . composed entirely of one single motive, the stubborn will to live." After her recovery she thinks that "her hardened, indifferent heart . . . had been tender and capable of love," but it is doubtful that she was ever capable of truly loving Adam, who appears as a projection of her desire to escape time, and of her fearful knowledge that she cannot escape, that she is doomed to grow old, lose her beauty, and die.

Miranda's concern for her appearance and her "uneasiness" at the first symptoms of influenza pertain directly to Adam's function as her double. She projects his "beauty" and perfect health because she desires eternal youth, but the reality of her situation ("I have pains in my chest and my head and my heart and they're real") causes her to transform him from a god into a time-doomed victim of her fears of old age and death. When Adam first greets Miranda, "She half noticed . . . that his smile faded gradually; that his eyes became fixed and thoughtful as if he were reading in a poor light." It is as if Adam's eyes become "fixed" in death. The word recurs twice more: his eyes are "fixed in a strained frown"; "his face [is] quite fixed and still." At the end of the same day Miranda completes his transformation from god to mortal as he sits in a restaurant "near the dingy big window, face turned to the street, but looking down. It was an extraordinary face, smooth and fine and golden in the shabby light, but now set in a blind melancholy, a look of pained suspense and disillusion. For just one split second she got a glimpse of Adam when he would have been older, the face of the man he would not live to be."

Miranda's glimpse of Adam grown old gives her a premonition of herself in the same condition. Having created his image out of her desire for immortality and then infected it with fear of aging, she finally denies him the aging process, as if his death were, paradoxically, a defense against the ravages of time. Her shifting images of him anticipate her own worst fears at the end of the story. His "blind melancholy" and "look of pained suspense and disillusion" precisely describe her mental state after her recovery from influenza. Even the "dingy" window and "shabby light" of the restaurant foreshadow the "melancholy wonder" of the hospital scene, "where the light seemed filmed with cobwebs, all the bright surfaces corroded. . . ." Miranda's physical transformation, wrought by disease, embodies all her earlier fears of aging. She is like one of the "old bedridden women down the hall," her trembling hands tinted "yellow . . . like melted wax glimmering between the closed fingers." It is as if she has aged as rapidly as she imagined Adam aging in the restaurant.

Miranda's narcissistic fear of aging also colors her views of those who have aged. We are less surprised than Adam at her overreaction to the bond salesman: "I hate these potbellied baldheads, too fat, too old, too cowardly, to go to war themselves. . . ." She also overreacts to Danny Dickerson, the pathetic has-been performer with his ten-year-old clippings: "He might have been a pretty fellow once, but now his mouth drooped where he had lost his side teeth, and his sad red-rimmed eyes had given up coquetry." Chuck doesn't understand why Miranda bothers to mention "the also-rans" in her reviews, nor would he understand the unconscious connection she has made between the "very beautiful" Adam and the once "pretty" Dickerson.

Miranda, then, projects Adam as dead or soon to die to protect herself from the engulfment of his love and to express her death wish through him. Identifying with him as good and mortal, she unconsciously wishes him dead because he reminds her of what will happen to her in time. Also, by removing him from time, she can preserve him as god and, at the end of the story, evoke him unchanged as "a ghost but more alive than she was." He becomes her "sacrificial lamb" because he enacts her death wish, allowing her to follow her stronger instinct of self-preservation.

Miranda's sexual fears also express her fears of engulfment and aging, as the symbolic relation between her influenza and her love of Adam suggests. Eleven days elapse between the couple's first meeting and the day influenza forces her to bed. Since the incubation period of the disease is from ten days to two weeks, her love and her disease develop simultaneously, although to Miranda "it seemed reasonable to suppose [her headache] had started with the war." Her flashback of the first nine days shows that she and Adam were frequently together without expressing any strong feeling for each other. But on the tenth day she is preoccupied with her love for him and with her malaise. She holds hands with him in the theater, apparently for the first time, and goes dancing with him: "They said nothing but smiled continually at each other, odd changing smiles as though they had found a new language." But their clearly expressed love is counterpointed against the Wasteland conversation of the girl at the next table who recounts her rejection of a former date's advances. In an abrupt transition we then discover Miranda in bed, gravely ill with influenza. But the point of the girl's rejection of her date is not lost, for Miranda sinks into her second dream which indirectly involves the rejection of her own date of the night before.

Miranda's second dream is a mixture of memory and delirium. She first evokes "cold mountains in the snow," the frigid Denver landscape of the present which she will associate, after her recovery, with deadened, loveless reality. She then evokes the past of her childhood, "another place she had known first and loved best," of warm skies, tropical trees and a "broad tranquil river," made slightly ominous by the "hovering buzzards." But this landscape suddenly changes into a hideous jungle, "a writhing terribly alive and secret place of death, creeping with tangles of spotted serpents, rainbow-colored birds with malign eyes . . . screaming long-armed monkeys tumbling among broad fleshy leaves that glowed with sulphur-colored light and exuded the ichor of death, and rotting trunks of unfamiliar trees sprawled in crawling slime." Miranda, waving gaily to herself in bed, enters the jungle and hears "the hoarse bellow of voices" warning her of danger and war.

As in the first dream Miranda's childhood landscape of warmth and security turns nightmarish, expressing her fear of the war and of life itself. First, the dream anticipates her death-in-life recovery from influenza, the "sulphur-colored light" of the leaves relating to the "sulphur colored light [that] exploded through the black window pane," and the exuding "ichor of death" relating to "the sweetish sickening smell of flesh and pus" of her body. The "hoarse bellow of voices all crying together, colliding above her head" is also picked up in the later passage: "Bells screamed all off key, wrangling together as they collided in mid air, horns and whistles mingled shrilly with cries of human distress. . . ." The voices in the dream cry of danger and war whereas the other voices are celebrating the Armistice, but for Miranda it is all the same: "the far clamor went on, a furious exasperated shrieking like a mob in revolt." Her nightmare of death is really her nightmare of life.

The jungle landscape also reveals Miranda's sexual fears. The "writhing terribly alive and secret place of death" reverses the connotations of the womb; life and death are juxtaposed because the "long march" to death, "beset with all evils" begins at birth. The phallic imagery in the passage suggests a terrifying version of the sex act. The seminal "ichor of death" and "crawling slime," extending the life-death paradox, relate to "the sweetish sickening smell of flesh and pus" of the passage describing her recovery because sex is a disease, just as marriage to the younger Miranda of "Old Mortality" is "an illness that she might one day hope to recover from."

The dream does not directly mention Adam although the phallic serpents may relate to his statement, "Where I'm going . . . [you] crawl about on your stomach here and there among the debris." However, this imagery shows that the prostrate Miranda unconsciously responds to his sexuality, her influenza an infectious accompaniment to her growing awareness of their love. After returning to her room after her dream, Adam, although "shy of the word *love*," finally tells Miranda that he loves her, his coat off, lying in bed with her, his arm under her shoulder and "his smooth face against hers," and "Almost with no warning, she floats into the darkness, holding his hand" only to dream of killing him. There is a causal relation between their intimacy and the content of her third dream.

Like the first two dreams the third is set in a wood, "an angry dangerous wood of inhuman concealed voices singing sharply like the whine of arrows," reminding us of the voices of the second dream and of the Armistice. Adam is struck in the heart by flights of arrows, but rises each time "in a perpetual death and resurrection," but when Miranda "selfishly" interposes between him and the arrows, they pass through her heart and kill him: ". . . he lay dead, and she still lived, and . . . every branch and blade of grass had its own terrible accusing voice."

The dream, as critics point out, expresses Miranda's guilt in exposing Adam to her contagion, but it also confirms the ambivalence of her love for him, seen earlier in her frequent predictions of his death. His "perpetual death and resurrection" repeat the pattern of her own escape from life to death to life, and again reveal her desire for immortality in her projection of him as a god, impervious to the onslaught of war and love. But again the image of the unchanging god gives way to Adam's human reality. His death, caused by her interposition, proves her own fear of endangering him by the contact of her love as well as her unconscious desire to escape his love by killing him. Laing points out that the insecure person "regards his own love and that of others as being destructive as hatred," causing him "to destroy 'in his mind' the image of anyone . . . he may be in danger of becoming fond of, out of a desire to safeguard that other person . . . from being destroyed." The bowdlerized version of the dream which Miranda gives Adam when she wakes—"There was something about an old-fashioned valentine" with "two hearts carved on a tree, pierced by the same arrow"—directly equates his death with the interlinking of their hearts. The arrows of her dream represent war, pestilence, love, and sexual contact. To Miranda they are all equally lethal.

When Adam leaves shortly after Miranda's third dream, he is replaced by Dr. Hildesheim, who carries her to the ambulance: " 'Put your arms around my neck,' he instructed her. 'It won't do any harm and it's a great help to me.' " His simulated affection and allusion to harm reinforce Miranda's ambivalence toward love, making him a fit substitute for Adam in the fourth dream. This dream, set in a "landscape of disaster," pictures Hildesheim as Boche, "his face a skull beneath his German helmet, carrying a naked infant writhing on the point of his bayonet" and a huge pot of poison. He throws the infant and poison into the "pure depths" of a once dry well on her father's farm, causing "the violated water" to sink back into the earth. Miranda emerges from her dream screaming, "Hildesheim is a Boche . . . kill him before he kills you."

This dream reveals Miranda's unconscious surrender to the war hysteria which she so abhors in her waking hours (the "baby on a bayonet" occurs in a Liberty Bond speech), but it also reveals hidden fears that existed before the war. Like the first two dreams it depicts Miranda's attempt to return to her childhood. Because he poisons her purified childhood memories and because his skull makes him another Pale Rider, Hildesheim is the enemy while Miranda is the baby whose retrogressive escape he prevents. Later she accuses him and others of conspiring "to set her once more safely in the road . . . to death." Whether projected as a monster by the unconscious or as well-meaning bungler by the conscious mind, Hildesheim is a scapegoat whom Miranda can conveniently blame, in her self-pity, for her unwillingness to accept her mortality.

The dream is also a condensation of Miranda's fearful version of life. Born naked into the world, helpless and pure as the living water of the well, she is subject to war (poison, bayonet), disease (poison), and death (skull), making Hildesheim as Hun and Pale Rider her enemy. Also subject to love and sex, equated with war and disease, she is "violated" by Hildesheim, a substitute for Adam and perhaps for all men. His phallic bayoneting recalls the Liberty Bond speech and Adam's earlier description of how he used the bayonet, gouging the "vitals" out of sandbags and watching the sand "trickling out," while the instructors cried, "Get him, get that Boche, stick him before he sticks you."

After her fourth dream Miranda's semi-conscious mind "split in two . . . her reasoning coherent self [watching] the strange frenzy of the other coldly, reluctant to admit the truth of its visions, its tenacious remorses and despairs." The splitting continues in a different form in the two main parts of her fifth dream. Both parts are extreme expressions of her isolation from life, yet completely opposite each other regarding the role her consciousness plays. In the first part she attempts to blot out experience by becoming insensate while in the second part she attempts to purify experience to make it conform to the dictates of her feelings.

In the first part Miranda, thinking about oblivion, finds herself "on a narrow ledge over a pit that she knew to be bottomless." When she is certain that "Death is death . . . and for the dead it has no attributes . . . she sank easily . . . until she lay like a stone at the farthest bottom of life, knowing herself to be blind, deaf, speechless, no longer aware of the members of her own body, entirely withdrawn from all human concerns. . . ." At this point she has dehumanized herself, "all ties of blood and the desires of the heart" dissolving and falling away from her except her "stubborn will to live."

Miranda is indeed at "the farthest bottom of life" physically and psychologically, her mind split away from her body and from her painful guilt over Adam and Hildesheim. It is her most extreme form of escape, an escape into nothingness in which she sheds her humanity and becomes an inanimate stone. Her struggle is best explained by Laing's comments: the insecure person, once he has successfully destroyed in his mind the image of anyone he loves and reduced all his wants to nothing, "sets about murdering his 'self.' . . . He descends into a vortex of nonbeing, but also to preserve being from himself." He notes elsewhere, ". . . to forgo one's autonomy becomes the means of secretly safeguarding it; to play possum, to feign death, becomes a means of preserving one's aliveness. To turn oneself into a stone becomes a way of not being turned into a stone by someone else."

The first part of Miranda's dream ends with her stubborn will to live, out of which springs her vision of a more hopeful and seemingly more human state of being. The setting is a "deep clear landscape of sea and sand, of soft meadow and sky," another landscape evoked from childhood memories, but with the difference that this one is peopled with "all the living she had known": "Their faces were transfigured . . . beyond what she remembered of them, their eyes were clear and untroubled . . . and they cast no shadows." Miranda later refers to this vision as "her paradise," "a child's dream of the heavenly meadow," but she has not envisioned an after-life, for eternity to her is "unknowable." Rather she has projected an idealized version of this life, where all the "living" are "transfigured," their "untroubled" eyes without the "awful expression of fear and suspicion" of which she had complained earlier. Yet all the living are so idealized that they are not human; they are "pure identities" who cast no shadows in a timeless world where it is "always morning." Miranda, "desiring nothing," "within touch but not touching" anyone, has purified human relationships out of existence in an attempt to render them harmless.

As her dream fades, Miranda resumes her painful journey back to life and death: she "felt without warning . . . some small flick of distrust in her joy . . . somebody was missing. . . . There are no trees, no trees here, she said in fright. . . . We have forgotten the dead, oh, the dead, where are they?" Some interpret this difficult passage to mean that Miranda has resisted death to return to Adam since later she complains, ". . . I wish you had come back, what do you think that I came back for, Adam, to be deceived like this?" But the passage states that she returns because the "somebody" missing from the "company of the living" is dead. And when she does return, she makes no inquiry about him; not until she reads many days later the letter informing her of his death, does she complain of being deceived.

The passage is better interpreted as part of the entire fifth dream, which moves downward to the farthest bottom of life and then upward and back to life. Miranda's vision of paradise is a stage between her desire to protect herself by turning into a stone, and her counter-desire to return to life, from which she has fled. Her paradise fades, as did her vision of Adam as god, because it is unreal and cannot be sustained. Having fled from life which threatens death to states of non-life too similar to death, she returns to life defined by the presence of death. Miranda needs the dead to know that she is alive despite the grief it causes her.

Miranda's need of the dead is symbolized by her alarm at the absence of trees in her dream of paradise, which "the same monotonous landscape of dulled evergreens" replaces. The evergreens are symbols of life in death like the woods in her first three dreams. The "angry dangerous wood" of the third dream in which she kills Adam is probably inspired by Belleau Wood, patriotically evoked by the hated Liberty Bond salesman, who prompts her to think, "What's the matter with you, why aren't you rotting in Belleau Wood? I wish you were. . . ."

After her recovery Miranda exhibits all the symptoms of Laing's insecure person. Awakening to the smell of death in her body, she thinks, "The body is a curious monster, no place to live in, how could anyone feel at home there? Is it possible I can ever accustom myself to this place?" To her "all objects and beings" are "meaningless, ah, dead and withered things that believed themselves alive!" She is "not quite dead now . . . one foot in either world," but she assures herself that she will "cross back and be at home again." "Condemned" to this life by those who have "conspired" to restore "her disordered mind," she views them with the "covertly hostile eyes of an alien." Although she knows that people will say that they love her, "her hardened, indifferent heart shuddered in despair at itself, because it had been tender and capable of love." Similarly, the insecure person feels "more dead than alive" and unable "to experience himself 'together with' others or 'at home in' the world"; he lives "in despairing aloneness and isolation," an incomplete person " 'split' in various ways, perhaps as a mind more or less tenuously linked to a body. . . ." Obviously, Miranda would not view herself in these terms since she feels fortified by a knowledge gained at a terrible price in her struggle with death in her fifth dream.

Miranda's vision of paradise is crucial to her view of herself and of the world. It confirms her despair of ever finding happiness, but it also reinforces her "stubborn will to live." Knowing that there is no escape from the world, she is stoically determined to live in it but not be part of it. She will disguise her face with make-up and mask her inward feeling with a smile so as not to "tamper with the courage of the living." Their courage is based on the illusion that happiness can exist, but her brush with death has given her an insight into the "truth" which they are not privileged to share. Thus her secret knowledge which she considered the source of her despair makes her unique in her own eyes. As she prepares to reenter the world in "the dazed silence that follows the ceasing of the heavy guns," she almost covets that despair because to her it defines a courage superior to that of the living.

Miranda's constricting fear of self and others does not allow me to accept her at her own estimate as Wayne Booth and some other critics do. Yet Porter's comments on her own experiences, which became the basis for "Pale Horse, Pale Rider," seem to justify their interpretation. She reports that while working for Denver's *Rocky Mountain News* in 1918, she almost died of the influenza that carried off her friend Alexander, who had nursed her in the first stages of her illness. During her illness she had a "vision" which eventually became Miranda's "dream of the heavenly meadow":

> It took me a long time to go out and live in the world again. I was really "alienated," in the pure sense. It was, I think, the fact that I really had participated in death, that I knew what death was, and had almost experienced it. I had what the Christians call the "beatific vision," and the Greeks called the "happy day," the happy vision just before death. Now if you have had that, and survived it, come back from it, you are no longer like other people, and there's no use deceiving yourself that you are.

We can never know to what extent Porter transformed her vision of 1918 into her fiction of 1938, or to what extent her fiction transformed, in the next thirty years, her conception of her original experience. She has so mythologized it that her account of her own return from the dead seems more literal and mystical than that suggested by Miranda's playful dialogue with herself: "Lazarus, come forth. Not unless you bring me my top hat and stick. Stay where you are then, you snob. Not at all, I'm coming forth." Yet the close identification between author and character allows the reader to view "Pale Horse, Pale Rider" as a personal statement of Porter's self-perception as artist. The biographical, as well as thematic, key to the story is the old spiritual that gives it its title. When Adam summarizes the many verses about the rider's carrying off the whole family including the lover, Miranda responds, "Death always leaves one singer to mourn. 'Death, . . . oh leave one singer to mourn—.'" Death grants character and author their wish. Allowing her her vision, he leaves Porter to mourn her loss in her art. "Pale Horse, Pale Rider" is her new spiritual, justifying her role as artist and assuaging her guilt over her survival at the cost of another. It may also justify her detachment from any who might come between her and the practice of her art, for she has made her priorities clear: "But this thing between me and my writing is the strongest bond I have ever had—stronger than any bond or any agreement with any human being or with any other work I've ever done."

The close identification between author and character seems to indicate that Porter consciously intended the reader's acceptance of Miranda's estimate of her vision. My interpretation runs counter to her intention on *this* point, and implies that Miranda's fears, to some extent, originated in the author's own. Porter's statement, "When I was a child, I was always running away," relates to Miranda's escape from her sleeping family in the first dream, and the alienation "in the pure sense" that Porter experienced after her vision may have been an extreme manifestation of a condition that unconsciously existed before her own exposure to war and influenza.

Porter's comments pertain to Miranda's vision, but other comments reinforce my reading that Miranda deceives herself into thinking that, like Juliet, she has returned to her beloved only to find that he has died in her service. Such a motive is in the best tradition of romantic love, on which Porter theorizes in a letter to her nephew in 1948. In "love at first sight," the lover

> is instantly transfigured with a light of such blinding *brilliance all natural attributes disappear* and are replaced by those usually associated with archangels at least. They are *beautiful, flawless* in temperament, witty, intelligent, charming, of such infinite grace, sympathy, and courage, I always wonder how they could have come from such absurdly inappropri-

ate families. . . . It is a disaster, in fact. We are in love and while it lasts—. . . . And when it is over. And when *I have recovered from the shock*, and . . . *put my mangled life in order*, I can then begin to remember what really happened. It is probably the silliest kind of love there is, but I'm glad. . . . there were times when I saw human beings at their best, for I don't think by any means that I lent them all their *radiance*. . . . Lightning makes the most *familiar landscape* wild, strange, and *beautiful*, and *it passes*. It was all my fault, though. If one ever treats a man as if he were an archangel, he can't ever, possibly, consent to being treated like a human being again. He cannot do it, it's nonsense to expect it. It begins to look as if I had never wanted it.

The words I have italicized recall Miranda's description of Adam, her dream of paradise, and her subsequent disillusion. The passage suggests that Miranda's very act of idealizing Adam is proof that she, like Porter, never wanted a lasting love relationship at all. Although Porter wrote her letter ten years after she published her story, she may have intended Miranda's self-deception. In an interview she remembered telling a friend in Mexico that Alexander was the only man she could have spent her life with. "And he replied, 'Just think, now he can never disappoint you.' And I suppose if there is anything at all good about it, that's it, but it does seem an awfully high price to pay to keep one's illusions, doesn't it?" Her friend, who could not have made his sardonic remark later than 1931, the last year of her stay in Mexico, exposed her self-deception which she had probably tried to sustain since her recovery from influenza. By 1938 she must have known that her attempt was futile. If she did intend that the reader accept Miranda's estimate of her love for Adam despite her own suspicions about Alexander and romantic love, her suspicions crept into her story nevertheless, as an examination of Miranda's dreams reveals.

Porter's near identification with Miranda illuminates but cannot resolve the problem of whether the reader should accept her at her own estimate, although it helps explain why critics are divided on the issue. In this paper we have viewed Miranda "from above" because we know more about her than she knows about herself, but that does not diminish the force of our sympathy for her as unwitting victim of overwhelming circumstances and of her ontologically insecure personality.

JOANN P. COBB

Pascal's Wager and
Two Modern Losers

Blaise Pascal addressed his argument of the wager to the seventeenth-century sceptic confronting the failure of reason to answer the question, "Does God exist?" Pascal in his zeal for conversion of the free-thinker intended the wager on the affirmative answer as only a last-ditch appeal to self-interest and as a predisposition for the infusion of faith, and modern opinion has been influenced by Voltaire's disparaging comment that it is indecent to introduce the concept of a game involving gain and loss to the grave subject of the existence of God. But three centuries later, the wager has a relevance to the society shaped by logical positivism and existential "angst" that has not been entirely overlooked. Two modern short stories present wagerers who lose: Granny Weatherall in Katherine Anne Porter's "The Jilting of Granny Weatherall" and The Misfit in Flannery O'Connor's "A Good Man Is Hard to Find." These contemporary gamblers illustrate an implication of the argument unexploited by Pascal, but the frequent inclusion of these stories in anthologies and textbooks testifies to the compelling pertinence of the "game."

The most appropriate position in the *Pensées* for the fragment containing the argument of the wager is still the subject of some debate, but most editors place it after Pascal has delineated the miseries of the human condition and the paradoxical status of mankind. A mixture of misery and greatness, man is endlessly frustrated: "We desire truth, and

From *Philosophy and Literature* 2, vol. 3 (Fall 1979). Copyright © 1979 by University of Michigan.

find within us naught but uncertainty. We seek happiness, and find only misery and death. We are incapable of not desiring truth and happiness, and are incapable of certainty or happiness." Man's greatness, for Pascal, consists in knowledge of his own misery as he confronts the human situation: "No great elevation of soul is needed to understand that here below is no true and solid satisfaction; that all our pleasures are but vanity, that our woes are infinite, and that lastly death, which threatens us every moment, must infallibly in a few years land us in the dreadful necessity of being forever either annihilated or miserable." Such understanding leads to thought of the Infinite, but "if there is a God, He is infinitely incomprehensible" and we are incapable of knowing by the light of nature "what He is, or whether He is."

Yet, Pascal says, "a game is on, at the other end of . . . infinite distance, and heads or tails will turn up." Pascal argues that man must wager for he is "embarked," and he cites the odds of the game's outcome as it will affect man's happiness: "Let us weigh gain and loss in calling heads that God is. Reckon these two chances: if you win, you win all; if you lose, you lose naught." Pascal secures the assent of the postulated listener with repeated assertions that the chances of success are even, while the possible gain is infinitely disproportionate to the stake. Pascal's "unbeliever" gives up without much fight, agreeing that he will wager though he cannot believe. In a much criticized passage, Pascal then prescribes the sceptic's course: seek a decrease of human passions, rather than an increase of divine proofs, make believe you believe by using the ritual of the Catholic religion, and this will bring you to believe. And Pascal repeats the question: "What have you to lose?"

Pascal's answer, of course, is "nothing" (rien), and he describes the attributes of the sceptic who follows the path of the believer: "You will be faithful, honest, humble, grateful, beneficent, a good friend, true. . . . I tell you that you will gain in this life, and that at every step you take on this road you will see such certainty of gain, such nothingness in what you risk, that you will at last realize that you have wagered on something certain and infinite, for which you have risked naught." But a modern reader is not so quick to agree that "naught" is at stake: "Unmoved by the apologist's disparagement of life on earth, knowing it to be more than rien and not wholly composed of 'plaisirs empestes,' he might contend that it is in any case far too precious to be staked in a once-for-all wager on an existence for which the chances, so far from being even, are in his judgment infinitely small." An interpretation more sympathetic to Pascal's rien sidesteps the issue by avoiding its immediate existential elements: "If God does not exist the atheist will have gained nothing because after his death he will disappear into the void and his life will be as though it had never been. The Christian will have lost nothing because he will no longer even be able to remember the pleasures which he has foregone."

The point at issue, however, in "The Jilting of Granny Weatherall" and "A Good Man Is Hard to Find" is the possibility of gain or loss in *this life*: this is the stake that is wagered. For if the full implications of Pascal's argument are extrapolated, he who wagers "God is" has nothing to lose in this life even if the coin falls "tails," while he who wagers "God is not" has nothing to gain in this life no matter which way the coin falls. While incidentally illustrating earthly consequences of the wager, Porter and O'Connor present dissimilar gamblers and contrasting conclusions about the eventual fall of the coin.

"The Jilting of Granny Weatherall" details the dying hours of eighty-year-old Ellen Weatherall. Through stream-of-consciousness narrative, the reader follows Granny's "rummaging around in her mind," as well as her responses to family, physician, and priest who come and go at her bedside. Granny Weatherall emerges as a salty-tongued, independent old woman, who refuses until the very end to give up her right to self-determination. While Granny's caustic comments betray an unsentimental view of her children (and physicians and priests) and perhaps an excess of that well-known parental syndrome, "Mother knows best," the very real love that flows both ways between mother and children is evident. Granny has "weathered" a long hard life and is justifiably proud of her accomplishments, but her passionate and successful determination to produce order out of chaos, "to spread out the plan of life and tuck in the edges orderly," has not eradicated that moment sixty years before when she stood on the edge of the abyss.

At the age of twenty, Ellen Weatherall was jilted on her wedding day when the bridegroom, George, failed to appear. Sixty years later, when she remembers that day, "a whirl of dark smoke rose and covered it, crept up and over into the bright field where everything was planted in orderly rows. That was hell, she knew hell when she saw it. For sixty years she had prayed against remembering him and against losing her soul in the deep pit of hell." This "hell" that she knows intimately seems necessarily to be the classic one of despair—loss of hope, belief, and trust in anything or anyone. Even now, sixty years later, the "sharp voice in the top of her mind" recalls the determination which helped her through that agony: "Don't let your wounded vanity get the upper hand of you. Plenty of girls get jilted. You were jilted, weren't you? Then stand up to it." The act of will which reduced hate and despair to "wounded vanity" signifies both courage and determination.

Ellen did "stand up to it" through marriage on the rebound to John, the husband she eventually came to love, through the single-handed rearing of the children after John's death at an early age, and through hard work and service to others: "Digging post holes changed a woman. Riding country roads in the winter when women had their babies was another thing: sitting up nights with sick horses and sick negroes and sick children and hardly ever losing one." Since that desperate wedding day, Ellen has waged war against loss, against chaos. In her passion for order, she has planned everything, and at age eighty she is worried about neither body nor soul. She brushes off the ministrations of Dr. Harry, for at age sixty she had decided she was finished, said good-bye to her children and grandchildren, had made a will, and had gone to bed with a fever. When she survived, she decided to forget about dying. And she cannot take Father Connolly seriously because "she felt easy about her soul."

Ellen's spiritual serenity derives from the decision made sixty years before: "She had her secret comfortable understanding with a few favorite saints who cleared a straight road to God for her. All as surely signed and sealed as the papers for the new Forty Acres. Forever . . . heirs and assigns forever. Since the day the wedding cake was not cut, but thrown out and wasted." On that day when she renounced despair, Ellen wagered her life on the existence of a more dependable bridegroom, and as she stares at the diminishing point of light that is herself being swallowed by the darkness, she awaits His coming: "God give a sign!"

> For the second time there was no sign. Again no bridegroom and the priest in the house. She could not remember any other sorrow because this grief wiped them all away. Oh, no, there's nothing more cruel than this—I'll never forgive it. She stretched herself with a deep breath and blew out the light.

Ellen's suicidal gesture has been interpreted as a refusal to surrender herself to the Infinite, but surely the contextual assertion should read: "God is not." If God is not, then Granny Weatherall placed her bet on the wrong side of the coin. She has lost, but what? Pascal's answer, "naught," applies in a way he never intended to Ellen Weatherall. She has not lost the Infinite, since in the context of the story there is none to lose. What she staked was her life on this earth, and what she achieved in that life is very likely the most that was possible. She comes across in the story as a woman of wit, humor, determination, and toughness. If she lacks the saccharine submission associated with "little old ladies," that is entirely to her credit. The need for her fiercely maintained independence was thrust upon her, she accepted the challenge, and she reveled in it.

Not everyone agrees, however, that Granny Weatherall is a character of significant stature. Some critics insist that Ellen Weatherall is a failure because she is sexually frigid, she rejects men, or that "she was 'unsuccessful' because she never again dared seek a love as vital as the one she was once cruelly denied. Rather she settled for the safer and seemingly less dangerous way of order." This reading of her character leads to the suspect conclusion that the second bridegroom, Christ, "denies her his presence for the same reason that George did—which is that He knows she does not really want Him." The loss that haunts Granny throughout her adult life then becomes a result of her own inadequacy or a "juvenile fixation on romance."

The obvious reply to these interpretations is that Ellen's "fixation" is less romantic than that recurring theory that a woman will achieve success and happiness only through total submission to a man. Though she assesses their relationship with the candor of old age, it is evident that Ellen learned to love John, the man who cursed like a sailor's parrot and caught her as she fainted after the first jilting. Her reference to the last child (Hapsy?) as the one "she had truly wanted. . . . Everything came in good time" surely reveals an acceptable depth of love. If she speaks of John as a child (another alleged symptom of her rejection of men), it is only because relative to her eighty years John was a boy when he died and she wonders how he will recognize her in the next life. She would like to believe that her life has been fulfilled, but she cannot. So she clings to the romantic illusion that George might have supplied that missing dimension: "Oh, no, God, no, there was something else besides the house and the man and the children. Oh, surely they were not all? What was it? Something not given back." If the assumption that George could have supplied the lack, already disproved by her life with John, is a "juvenile fixation," it should be remembered that in this story the hope that Christ will fulfill that need is equally a romantic illusion.

Yet the need is there, and ironically it is this hunger for something not achievable on the human plane that is one of Pascal's most telling arguments for the necessity of the wager:

> We sail over a vast expanse, ever uncertain, ever adrift, carried to and fro. To whatever point we think to fix and fasten ourselves it shifts and leaves us; and if we pursue it, it escapes our grasp, slips away, fleeing in eternal flight. Nothing stays for us. This is our condition, natural, yet most contrary to our inclination; we have a burning desire to find a sure resting place and a final fixed basis whereupon to build a tower to the Infinite; but our whole foundation cracks, and the earth yawns to the abyss.

Granny Weatherall's accommodation to the human condition that Pascal describes is order. Her determination to make her life meaningful despite her real experience with the slippery basis of human relationships attains significant, though finite, success. If, as Katherine Anne Porter suggests, this life is all there is, then its value derives from how it is lived and what remains after. Granny has been a successful mother, a compassionate neighbor, and her children remain as a testament to her achievement. If she realizes that this is not enough to reach complete happiness, that is a long-recognized condition of human existence. If her belief in happiness after death rests on another "cracked foundation," that is simply the chance that everyone takes.

But her alternative, as Granny well knows, is Hell. By staking her life and the way she lived it on the hope of a better life hereafter, Granny Weatherall lost nothing. The despair that tempted her after the first jilting creates a Hell on earth while it risks Hell in the next world. And Flannery O'Connor's Misfit illustrates the consequences of that choice.

"A Good Man Is Hard to Find" is the first in a collection of O'Connor short stories also carrying that title. In her own words, "A Good Man Is Hard to Find' is "the story of a family of six which, on its way driving to Florida, gets wiped out by an escaped convict who calls himself The Misfit. The family is made up of the Grandmother and her son, Bailey, and his children, John Wesley and June Star and the baby, and there is also the cat and children's mother. The cat is named Pitty Sing, and the Grandmother is taking him with them, hidden in a basket." This bare-bones sketch of the plot enervates, of course, the richly textured story with its humor, horror, and pathos. But it serves to isolate the relative importance of the characters. The story is the grandmother's, though that is the only name she is ever given. Bailey, her son, is a stolid man who says little, the children are brats, and the cat has more character than the children's mother. Essentially, it is the story of the grandmother's confrontation with The Misfit.

The grandmother is a superficial and irritating woman who prides herself on being a "lady." Through her zany manipulations, the family takes a road which it should never have tried, the cat which she has stowed away causes an accident, and the family confronts The Misfit. The grandmother, who condemns the family when she identifies The Misfit, undertakes with her typical lack of comprehension to talk him out of killing her: " 'You wouldn't shoot a lady, would you. . . . Listen,' the grandmother almost screamed, 'I know you're a good man. You don't look a bit like you have common blood. I know you must come from nice people!' " And as The Misfit's companions systematically exterminate the rest of her family, the grandmother elicits the story of his life.

The Misfit agrees that he comes from "nice people," and he exemplifies the grandmother's definition of "nice," i.e., "good": he tries to explain that Bailey didn't really mean the unprintable epithet he aimed at his mother after she identified The Misfit, he politely talks about the weather, and he apologizes for being improperly dressed before "ladies." But, at the same time, he is inviting the rest of her family off to the woods for execution. Finally, The Misfit asserts that he is not a "good man," but he insists that he is not the worst either: "My daddy said I was a different breed of dog from my brothers and sisters. 'You know,' Daddy said, 'it's some that can live their whole life out without asking about it and it's others has to know why it is, and this boy is one of the latters.' " The Misfit insists that he was not a "bad boy," but somehow he got sent to the penitentiary: "I was buried alive." The Misfit cannot remember his crime, though he admits "a head-doctor at the penitentiary said what I had done was kill my daddy but I known that for a lie." The grandmother urges him to pray to Jesus for help but The Misfit replies, "I don't want no hep . . . I'm doing all right by myself." And he continues his reverie: "I found the crime don't matter. You can do one thing or you can do another, kill a man or take a tire off his car, because sooner or later you're going to forget what it was you done and just be punished for it." This is his justification for his pseudonym: "I call myself The Misfit because I can't make what all I done wrong fit what all I gone through in punishment."

Thus The Misfit, in his own bizarre way, reflects the conflict of every person who has to know "why life is." His basic complaint against human existence is undeserved "punishment." The familiar metaphor of life as a "prison" gives one justification for The Misfit's behavior, but he proves to be more than just another rationalizing outlaw. He too has recognized the need for the Pascalian wager. After the grandmother has called to her dead son to return from the woods, The Misfit reveals his understanding of the gamble:

> "Jesus was the only One that ever raised the dead . . . and He shouldn't have done it. He thown everything off balance. If he did what He said, then it's nothing for you to do but thow away everything and follow Him, and if He didn't, then it's nothing for you to do but enjoy the few minutes you got left the best way you can—by killing somebody or burning down his house or doing some other meanness to him. No pleasure but meanness," he said and his voice had become almost a snarl.

That snarl reduces the hysterical grandmother to apostasy: " 'Maybe He didn't raise the dead,' the old lady mumbled." But, as usual, she misses the point:

> "I wasn't there so I can't say He didn't," The Misfit said. "I wisht I had of been there," he said, hitting the ground with his fist. "It ain't right I wasn't there because if I had of been there I would of known. Listen lady," he said in a high voice, "if I had of been there I would of known and I wouldn't be like I am now."

His suffering provokes the grandmother's well-documented "moment of grace," in which she reaches out to him in real compassion. The Misfit's reaction—he shoots her three times through the chest—is predictable, but he has established his claim to humanity: he has recognized the need to know and to choose.

As a Pascalian gambler, The Misfit chooses to believe, or to act as if he believes, that "Jesus didn't do what He said." His agnosticism dictates his choice of "tails": since he cannot know that "God is," he stakes his life that "God is not." He risks eternal loss if the coin falls "heads" (and in the context of the story it does), in exchange for this life's pleasure. But this life's "pleasure" turns out to be "naught." After the grandmother's death, one of the other murderers chortles: "Some fun!" But The Misfit has the last word: " 'Shut up, Bobby Lee,' The Misfit said. 'It's no real pleasure in life.' "

Admittedly, The Misfit is a psychotic and atypical representative of believers in the pleasure principle, but his recognition of the need to wager and the risk he is willing to take establish his claim to humanity. The Misfit asserts his human freedom by his will to live according to his choice. In contrast, the members of the grandmother's family seem hardly alive. And the grandmother becomes truly human only in her moment of recognition of The Misfit's suffering. Taken together the grandmother and The Misfit illustrate opposite extremes of Pascal's dictum: "To know God without knowing his own misery, and to know his own misery without knowing God, are equal dangers for man." The grandmother's superficial and "ladylike" Christianity became true knowledge of God only when she recognized man's misery, while The Misfit had terrible experience of human misery, but was unable to acknowledge God. As Pascal explains it, "Knowledge of God without knowledge of our misery begets pride. Knowledge of our misery without knowledge of God begets despair. Knowledge of Jesus Christ strikes the balance, because in Him we discover both God and our misery." Ironically, The Misfit in his despair believes that Jesus "thown everything *off balance*."

The grandmother's moment of enlightenment: "Why you're one of my babies. You're one of my own children," illustrates another Pascalian theme. Pascal repeatedly refers to the "hidden God" (*le Dieu caché*), but he insists that every man has the opportunity to know the existence of God. "There is light enough to enlighten the elect, and darkness enough to humble them. There is darkness enough to blind the reprobates and light enough to damn them and render them inexcusable." That one moment of recognition apparently ensures the grandmother's salvation: the dead grandmother "half sat and half lay in a puddle of blood with her legs crossed under like a child's and her face smiling up at the cloudless sky." That same moment of light damns her adversary: "The Misfit sprang back as if a snake had bitten him and shot her three times through the chest. Then he put his gun down on the ground and took off his glasses and began to clean them."

Though the permanent efficacy of the grandmother's one act of understanding strains the imagination, The Misfit has been consistent throughout. If the grandmother's ultimate position signifies her reward after death, the coin will fall "heads" and The Misfit is a double loser: he has lost the chance of infinite bliss as well as the possibility of limited happiness on this earth. He has lost everything and gained "naught." In his despair, he has created his own Hell on earth: "It's no real pleasure in life."

The Misfit's choice of "meanness" in response to the unknowable is significant because it is a *choice*. And choice is required of all those who are not content to "live their whole life out without asking about it." Implicit in The Misfit's acknowledgement of the necessity of question and choice is Flannery O'Connor's existential commitment: without choice the human being is nothing, as the grandmother is nothing until her moment of recognition and choice. That even the correct (in O'Connor's view) choice will prove fatal, on the human plane at least, is an unalterable fact of human existence. This tragic view of human life and the existential commitment to choice undergird the disparate approaches of Pascal, Porter, and O'Connor. All three assert the chaotic transcience experienced by human beings who long for order and permanence. And all three celebrate the human freedom to choose order and permanence.

Pascal's insistence that one cannot avoid wagering has been called "prophetic of existentialism," an existentialism which would accept the necessity of choice but not his either/or response to Christian theism. Yet the response *is* essentially either/or, translated perhaps from Pascal's "God is/is not" to the contemporary "Meaning is/is not." Katherine Anne Porter expresses her choice in terms of her artistic practice of exercising her "natural tendency to try to wangle the sprawling mess of our existence in this bloody world into some kind of shape: almost any shape will do, just so it is recognizably made with human hands, one small proof the more of the validity and reality of the human imagination." Porter's belief in the value of the human imagination is a positive assertion: life is meaningful. And she recognizes her affinity with Pascal: "The silence of the spaces between the stars does not affright me, as it did Pascal, because I am unable to imagine it except poetically; and my awe is not for the silence and space of the endless universe but for the inspired imagination of man, who can think and feel so, and turn a phrase like that to communicate it to us." Porter's awe at the *inspired* imagination which can shape the "sprawling mess of our existence in this bloody world" is tantamount to a wager that "God (Meaning/Truth/Eternity) is."

To capitulate to the "sprawling mess" is to despair. Exemplified antithetically in Granny Weatherall's passion for order, despair becomes, in Porter's story, the loss of belief in the value of human existence lived in accord with some moral standard. Despair does not require the murderous paranoia exhibited by O'Connor's Misfit. It can exist in the refusal to endow human life with meaning or, as Kierkegaard puts it, in living as the majority of men do "without being thoroughly conscious that they are spiritual beings." Those who choose to believe in nothing—and to act upon that belief—wager in fact that "God (Meaning/Truth/Eternity) is not," and they must lose, for they will find only meaninglessness and disorder.

Those who value the human spirit, however, can only "win." Whether that "spirit" is acknowledged as the supernatural destiny of Pascal and O'Connor or the shaping imagination of Porter, belief in its value commits one to that moral order which is meaningful on this earth, and perhaps in some larger context as well.

In the face of the unknown it is prudent, Pascal tells us, to place our bets where there is the greatest possibility of gain. The game is on, we are engaged, and we must wager. Those who wager "God is" have everything to gain and nothing to lose.

BRUCE W. JORGENSEN

"The Other Side of Silence": Katherine Anne Porter's "He" as Tragedy

"**H**e" ends as Mrs. Whipple is taking her feeble-minded, unnamed son to the County Home where she has finally admitted He may receive better care and no longer physically burden his family for whom "Life was very hard." [*The Collected Stories of Katherine Anne Porter* (New York: Harcourt Brace Jovanovich, 1965), p. 49. Subsequent references will be documented parenthetically by page number]. On the way He begins to cry, "rubbing His nose with His knuckles, and then with the end of the blanket" and "scrubbing away big tears that rolled out of the corners of His eyes" (p. 58). Neither we nor Mrs. Whipple can know for certain the motive of His weeping, but it drives in upon His mother the awareness she has warded off all of His life—that, however hindered by His condition from showing love or gratitude, He is far more a human being, a person, than she has allowed herself to think. The knowledge is terrible; whatever the reason for His weeping,

> Mrs. Whipple couldn't bear to think of it. She began to cry, frightfully, and wrapped her arms tight around Him. His head rolled on her shoulder: she had loved Him as much as she possibly could, there were Adna and Emly who had to be thought of too, there was nothing she could do to make up to Him for His life. Oh, what a mortal pity He was ever born.

From *Modern Fiction Studies* 3, vol. 28 (Autumn 1982). Copyright © 1982 by Purdue Research Foundation.

> They came in sight of the hospital, with the neighbor driving
> very fast, not daring to look behind him.

Miss Porter once remarked that "Any true work of art has got to
give you the feeling of reconciliation—what the Greeks would call catharsis, the purification of your mind and imagination—through an ending
that is endurable because it is right and true. . . . Sometimes the ending is
very tragic, because it needs to be." The ending of "He," I believed when
I first tried to discuss the story with beginning literature students, intends
just such a catharsis, "endurable because it is right and true" and "tragic
because it needs to be." Surely the last two sentences intend to focus for
our minds and imaginations the classic emotions that Aristotle said tragedy purifies— pity and terror; and surely those emotions are proper to the
situation and action of "He."

My students had a hard time seeing it: either they excessively,
sentimentally pitied Mrs. Whipple, or they excessively, moralistically condemned her. I have since learned that recent critics of Miss Porter's story
have fared little better: most of them lean either toward excessive pathos
or toward excessive, even contemptuous irony. Thus James W. Johnson in
1960, though mentioning "the unavoidable tragedy of the abnormal child,
the victim of a biological accident" (thus seeming to use the word in its
loose, non-literary sense of "deep misfortune"), moralistically implied that
Mrs. Whipple might have suffered less had she not "refus[ed] to accept the
facts." Harry John Mooney came a little closer in 1962, speaking of the
"pathetic ending" as a "final" and "grim tragedy in a mother's life" and of
the story itself as "a small tragedy"; but he did not point to the pity and
terror of the ending as evidence, nor did he explain what he meant, and
he sentimentalized Mrs. Whipple in seeing her as "altogether committed
to Him." In 1963 Paul F. Deasy, though seeing that in the last scene Mrs.
Whipple realizes "He is as real as anybody," read the story moralistically as
showing how Mrs. Whipple's "failure to face reality leads to frustration";
he saw her love for her child as "unreal" and argued, without explaining
how, that "Peace would lie in accepting Him as He is."

William L. Nance in 1964 viewed the story as "a masterpiece of
finely balanced satire and pathos" with an "all-judging ironic narrator"; he
found no one in the story "with whom the author or reader is inclined to
identify sympathetically," and like Deasy he condemned Mrs. Whipple's
"totally inadequate response to reality," her "folly of self-delusion" or
"willful blindness"; he rightly called attention to "the failure of the boy's
parents to recognize his personality" as "the root of their error and
suffering" but also, without evidence, blamed their poverty on "their own

laziness and ineptitude"; though finally allowing that the last scene "leaves the reader suspended between condemnation and sympathy for this weak woman in her hard fate," he seemed to miss the way the last sentence about the driver brings into focus the tragic emotion of terror.

In 1965, George Hendrick saw the story as "stressing the irony of the situation but ending with compassion for both mother and child," yet he did not allow that the reader could have compassion for Mrs. Whipple before the end; he felt, rightly I think, that the boy is "beyond human help," able to "receive but . . . not [to] return love"; yet far too simplistically he saw Mrs. Whipple's "professed love" as merely "a cover for hatred" thinly masked "with Christian piety"; for him, finally, the story was "completely pessimistic." Winfred S. Emmons in 1967 allowed the Whipples "a certain dignity, though small," and admitted the boy was "a problem that nobody could solve"; but he also saw Mrs. Whipple as "very possibly hat[ing] Him," as certainly "wish[ing] He had never been born" (though that is not precisely what she says), and as practicing "the eleventh commandment, which is to put up the appearance of a virtue if you cannot manage the real thing"; for him, the story's tone was "unrelievedly pathetic."

In 1971, in the fullest discussion so far, Myron M. Liberman called "He" one of the most "harrowing" stories in English, "a little gem of enormous thematic magnitude" in which "a universe of human suffering is worked out . . . in a way that involves the reader most painfully, without resorting to sentimentality or preachment," and in which the author "succeeds as always in maintaining that 'delicate balance of rival considerations' " that Robert Penn Warren long ago cited as a primary quality of her work; like Hendrick, Liberman saw the ironic narrative voice as allowing the reader to feel compassion for Mrs. Whipple only at the end; reading more cautiously than Hendrick or Emmons, he noted that "no matter how His mother feels about Him, that feeling is bound to be something less than unalloyed love," yet he did not clearly define her feeling; he did see what I would call the "choral" function of the last sentence about the neighbor, and thus came close to defining the story's catharsis; most importantly, he pointed out that "the burden of the story is the terrible question of how many of us could have succeeded in giving love where Mrs. Whipple failed."

That remark, of course, is the perfect answer to those critics who find it too easy to condemn Mrs. Whipple, and after Liberman's care and clarity it is a letdown to come to John Edward Hardy's comment in 1973 (which acknowledged a debt to Liberman's discussion of the neighbor's final reaction), for Hardy saw Mrs. Whipple as having an "obsession" with her retarded son which she is "pleased to call . . . love"; he regarded her as "severely punished" in the end for the "cruel folly" of her pride; thus he found it "easy justice on the reader's part to refuse [Mrs. Whipple the pity] she so despises."

The main irony of the critical history of "He" is that its earliest commentators, those of the Thirties and Forties, read the story most clearly, whereas those of the Sixties and Seventies, supposedly better trained, have so persistently misconstrued it or seen it partially rather than as a whole. Thus Mary Orvis in 1948 saw Mrs. Whipple as "caught in a moral trap" from which "there is in all reality no possible escape" and in which her final action "is at best a compromise that must confront her all the rest of her life," leaving her "only the agony of guilt." Mrs. Orvis did not use the word "tragedy" in her comment, yet she defined the story clearly in a way that would accord with Karl Jaspers' dictum, "Absolute and radical tragedy means that there is no way out whatsoever." Claude M. Simpson and Allan Nevins in 1941 also viewed the ending of the story as "an incident of genuine tragedy," though without explaining why. But surely the most accurate comment on the story was the earliest, Howard Baker's single paragraph published in 1938, which used "He" to represent Miss Porter's "remarkable attainment" in *Flowering Judas*, her "perfection of a highly selective realistic method": viewing the retarded boy as "a kindly, helpful, and beloved creature, whom his parents cannot avoid taking advantage of, and who exceeds little by little their capacity for caring for him," Baker saw how the author was able "to indicate fully the thousand-fold aspects of the parents' predicament—the love, the misgivings, the rationalizings, the blind hope, the impotence, the awareness of need for help, the shame at having the neighbors know"—in such a way that "the story becomes genuinely tragic."

The problem "He" poses for its audience, critics and common readers alike, is moral as much as literary: how to avoid easy pity or easy contempt for Mrs. Whipple; how to arrive at the justice of a clear, balanced estimate of her situation, character, and actions. Baker's summary displays the kind of critical negative capability that the problem demands—the capacity to see Mrs. Whipple in terms of both/and rather than either/or, to see that she can and does love her retarded son even at the same time she compulsively exposes Him to danger and harm, and to see that intolerable moral paradox as defining her tragic predicament. Baker took a long step forward in understanding the story, which unfortunately most recent critics failed to follow. Those who saw Mrs. Whipple's love as a mere mask for her "real" hatred and thus found it easy to condemn her would have done well to take the advice Blake once addressed in a couplet "To God":

> If you have form'd a Circle to go into,
> Go into it yourself & see how you would do.

Liberman at least brought the discussion back to this point.

The audience's problem with Mrs. Whipple, I suspect, was also the author's problem, and I further suspect that she began to solve it by going into the circle she had formed, sympathetically trying to see Mrs. Whipple's situation from inside, though with greater clarity of intelligence than Mrs. Whipple could possibly bring to bear on it. We might formulate the moral problem Mrs. Whipple faces in this way: because her son is retarded (and after a head injury forgets the few words He has learned), so that He cannot respond to His family or express His feelings with anything approaching the fullness of even relatively inarticulate people like the Whipples, He is in some sense hindered from being fully a person, but He is not a dumb animal either. Mrs. Whipple must in the beginning have loved Him as instinctively as most parents love the infants who must utterly depend on them; but as His body grew, He remained in that infantile dependence, and Mrs. Whipple already had one child older than He, and later another younger, both of whom were normal and who thus not only outgrew their total dependence but also were capable of returning their parents' affection and of responsibly caring for some of their own needs. In the family's "hard" life (which, significantly, Miss Porter defines for us before introducing their second son), Mrs. Whipple cannot possibly care adequately for all three, so she compromises, giving Him a larger share of privation and risk because "He don't really mind" (p. 51); in this, of course, her judgment is already distorted by unconscious resentment of His disability and by guilt for that resentment. And so the fabric of Mrs. Whipple's self-deceptions and rationalizations weaves around her to the point where she cannot, until the end, realize or admit the degree to which He is a person. How *would* we do in that circle?

The great risk to our justice as we enter the circle is the temptation of sentimental identification with Mrs. Whipple, of excessive pity for her as the victim of impossible circumstances. The audience, and I suspect the author as well, needed some check on compassion, and the ironic narrative voice provides that check. Contra Hendrick and Liberman, I do not hear Miss Porter's irony as consistent throughout the story up to its last scene; to my ear its effects are intermittent, local rather than pervasive, and qualified by context so as not entirely to undercut Mrs. Whipple's view of herself.

Thus in the story's exposition we first see how Mrs. Whipple's stubborn, petty pride motivates the duplicity she practices "when the neighbors were in earshot" (p. 49); but with a retarded child and *those* neighbors, how would we do? For they talk "plainly among themselves" of how the child's defect is "the sins of the fathers," the result of "bad blood and bad doings somewhere, you can bet on that" (pp. 49–50). We can hardly blame Mrs. Whipple for not wanting to be looked down on by such neighbors, even if she doesn't know exactly what they say behind her back.

Similarly, that Mrs. Whipple is "forever saying" that she loves "her second son . . . better . . . than the other two children put together" and occasionally "even throw[ing] in her husband and her mother for good measure" (p. 49) does not necessarily mean that she simply hates her son. Mr. Whipple, bitter and cynical as he is, implicitly accepts that she does have "feelings about Him" (p. 49). As she says, "It's natural for a mother" (p. 49), and we need not deny her natural affection, even as we see that because it is also "expected," she exaggerates its quantity and purity and thus makes it increasingly difficult for herself to know her own true feelings.

Again, it seems quite true that, at one level, Mrs. Whipple "wouldn't have anything happen to Him for all the world" (p. 50), though this masks her unadmitted guilt over His defect and her suppressed resentment at His passive dependence. She does patently overstate His invulnerability ("He can do anything and not get a scratch"), and she takes a desperate though quite real and deep solace in the preacher's saying that "The innocent walk with God" (p. 50). In the incident of the plank striking His head, the irony is heavy and lucid: clearly He was injured, for "He had learned a few words, and after this He forgot them"; but it may also be simply true that "He never seemed to know it" (p. 50). We arrive at the same sort of judgment when "in bad weather" the Whipples give Emly "the extra blanket off His cot," rationalizing that "He never seemed to mind the cold" (p. 50); obviously it cannot be good for Him, yet He may indeed not "mind" it. It must be simply true that, however much she deceives herself about such compromies, "Just the same, Mrs. Whipple's life was a torment for fear something might happen to Him" (p. 50); but the torment must be compounded almost unimaginably by her fear of the neighbors' judgment, by her unacknowledged hostilty and by her guilt over it.

In the exposition of "He," then, an ironic narrative voice, always qualified by context so as to preclude easy, simplistic condemnation, requires us to make such complex judgments, allowing the validity of Mrs.

Whipple's natural motherly feelings but also insisting on the reality of her unadmitted guilt and hostility. Miss Porter was not the kind of writer who, in Arthur Mizener's words, "encourage[s] people to enjoy the insidious pleasures of righteousness unearned by understanding" by pretending she and her reader "are Christ harrowing a hell full of all the people who disagree with them"; the hell she imagines in "He" is not for other people, but for herself and her readers, too. And Miss Porter's irony—certainly in this story—is not a headsman's axe but a weight in the scale of justice to keep mercy from overtipping the balance. It serves to maintain a clear vision of Mrs. Whipple's flaws and errors and also to prevent the excess of pity that could blind a reader to her very real self-deceptions and to her internal conflicts, including the complicated guilt that corrodes her love for her son.

Throughout "He," except in the last paragraphs where it is no longer needful, that kind of irony operates from time to time, counterpoising Mrs. Whipple's professed feelings by clarifying her unacknowledged ones, as the story's action unfolds in a well-knit plot comprising three main episodes: the pig slaughtered to feast Mrs. Whipple's brother and his family; He leading a neighbor's bull to pasture at the Whipples' as payment for the bull's breeding their cow; His final removal to the County Home. In the first, Mrs. Whipple's pride brings her to endanger her son to serve its turn, and it also leads her toward a possible recognition of His personality and of her guilt: "When He saw the blood" as she slit the pig's throat, "He gave a great jolting breath and ran away" (p. 52); but Mrs. Whipple only thinks "He'll forget and eat plenty" and—probably correctly, though it is another rationalization—"He'd eat it all if I didn't stop Him" (p. 52). (At the meal, He won't enter the dining room where the pig lies in the center of the table, but presumably He does eat the "big plate" that Mrs. Whipple serves Him in the kitchen.) When on Sunday morning she boxes His ears for getting dirty, "His face hurt[s her] feelings," and her suppression of this incipient realization makes her physically weak (p. 53). The episode ends in despair for Mrs. Whipple ("—oh, honest, sometimes I wish I was dead!") but with no clarification because she is so full of self-pity (p. 54).

The Whipples' hardship the following winter comes partly from the improvident slaughter of the pig, which would have meant "three hundred pounds of pork" to use or to sell; with poor crops, they have barely enough money for food and thus too little for clothes. Most of that goes to Adna and Emly; because "He sets around the fire a lot, He won't need so much" (p. 54). He almost gets pneumonia, and, although He seems well next spring, "He walked as if His feet hurt Him" (p. 55)—probably a sign of some residual infection. The bull episode that summer develops from Mr. Whipple's effort to save "paying out money when [he hasn't] got it" (p. 55), and it once again reveals the intensity of Mrs. Whipple's moral and emotional conflicts. At first she feels "easy in her mind about sending Him for the bull," but then she starts thinking, "and after a while she could hardly bear it any longer" (p. 55). He returns, "leading the big bulk of an animal by a ring in his nose, . . . never looking back or sideways, but coming on like a sleepwalker with His eyes half shut" (p. 55) in what could be either near-paralyzing fear or just simple-minded insouciance. Mrs. Whipple possibly exaggerates the danger, for the bull lumbers "along behind Him as gently as a calf" (p. 56), but she recalls "awful stories about how [bulls] followed on quietly enough, and then suddenly pitched on with a bellow and pawed and gored a body to pieces," and she thinks how "Any second now that black monster would come down on Him" (p. 55). She imagines this so vividly that, when the bull harmlessly "horn[s] the air at a fly," she involuntarily shrieks, almost precipitating the violence that she fears and perhaps at the same time unconsciously desires. For her this episode ends in a frantic, self-serving prayer and nervous prostration, yet again without any recognition because her fear is so self-centered: "Lord, you *know* people will say we oughtn't to have sent Him. You *know* they'll say we didn't take care of Him. Oh, get Him home, safe home, safe home, and I'll look out for Him better! Amen" (p. 56).

The recognition does come in the final episode—a *peripeteia* and *anagnorisis* as close to the classical tragic pattern as anyone has ever come in a realistic short story. Mrs. Whipple is hardly a classical tragic heroine. Perhaps she hardly reaches the stature of Arthur Miller's "common man" who becomes tragic in being "ready to lay down his life, if need be, to secure one thing—his sense of personal dignity": one might say she destroys her integrity to maintain a partly specious sense of dignity. Yet her final tragic recognition, like that of Oedipus, does fall on her because of her most important traits of character, which have conflicted throughout the story—her quite genuine feeling for her son and her pride (she refuses the ambulance because she "couldn't stand to see Him going away looking so sick as all that," and when she rides with Him, she wears her most dignified "black shirt waist" because "she couldn't stand to go looking like charity" [p. 58]). In sending Him to the hospital, the Whipples simply intend His good, though his going will relieve them of practical burdens they can no longer bear (they can neither care well enough for Him themselves nor pay for the doctor's care; to keep Him would simply mean worsening poverty and privation, which could do Him no good). Yet, in a powerful situational irony, He weeps at what is happening, and there is no way Mrs. Whipple can ignore it or attribute it to anything except her present or past actions. The story's closing tableau is a devastating Pietá as the mother holds and weeps over her son, whose well-being and whose humanity she has continually sacrificed piecemeal to her confused feelings, and whose well-intentioned sacrificial expulsion now brings illumination but no release from guilt.

The cathartic ending of "He," "tragic because it needs to be" and "endurable because it is right and true," calls to mind a passage from Chapter Twenty of *Middlemarch*, in which George Eliot says,

> That element of tragedy which lies in the very fact of frequency, has not yet wrought itself into the coarse emotion of mankind; and perhaps our frames could hardly bear much of it. If we had a keen vision and feeling of all ordinary human life, it would be like hearing the grass grow and the squirrel's heart beat, and we should die of that roar which lies on the other side of silence. As it is, the quickest of us walk about well wadded with stupidity.

Miss Porter's subject in "He," tightly circumscribed by the Whipples' hard life and the ineludible moral dilemma of their feeble-minded son, is simply the tragic nature of ordinary familial love, of which, as she wrote twenty years after the story, "hatred is part . . . the necessary enemy and ally." With a keen vision and feeling of that ordinary love in her ordinary characters, the last scene of Miss Porter's story shows Mrs. Whipple finally hearing the roar on the other side of her son's inarticulate silence and of her own self-deceiving silence as well; it shows the terrified neighbor hearing both those roars; and it has the reader hearing all three in full fidelity. No one in our century has put the short story to nobler use—or to stricter discipline—than Katherine Anne Porter, and "He," a compact tragedy in the low mimetic mode of realistic fiction, is simply one of the finer instances of that fact: a classic story written "with all the truth and tenderness and severity" that Miss Porter intended as the hallmark of all her work.

DEBRA A. MODDELMOG

Narrative Irony and Hidden Motivations in Katherine Anne Porter's "He"

"He" has received varied critical attention in the fifty-five years since its publication, so varied in fact that the interpretations of its critics make one wonder whether they have read the same story. "He" is ostensibly about the Whipple family, but because Porter develops in detail only the relationship between Mrs. Whipple and her retarded son, the story becomes essentially a study of the psychology of that relationship. Critically, the key question seems to be how Porter wants the reader to react to Mrs. Whipple. Are we to view her finally with compassion, condemnation, or ambivalence?

Winfred Emmons, for example, says of the story's conclusion: "Everybody has done his best, but He was a problem that nobody could solve. The reader may hope that Mrs. Whipple's bright outlook will somehow return; it has seemed to be her natural state and would doubtless be more pleasant to her than the defeated pragmatism of her husband. And it is possible that their luck might change for the better some day. Sometimes luck works that way, and Mrs. Whipple's desire for order and a better life might find a way to help luck along." But whereas Emmons applauds Mrs. Whipple's optimism, William Nance claims that Mr. Whipple's main function in the story is "to furnish a welcome contrast to his wife by acting as the laconic voice of plain truth." And whereas Emmons

From *Modern Fiction Studies* 3, vol. 28 (Autumn 1982). Copyright © 1982 by Purdue Research Foundation.

·hopes that Mrs. Whipple's life will improve now that He has been placed in the county home, Nance takes a more ambivalent attitude toward the mother. He maintains that the reader is left "suspended between condemnation and sympathy for this weak woman in her hard fate." In contrast to Emmons and Nance, George Hendrick states that "He" ends with compassion for both the mother and the child, but that it is "a completely pessimistic story."

What gives rise to this diversity of opinion? M. M. Liberman suggests that "He" is a "gem of enormous thematic magnitude" and "a masterpiece of compression" in the tradition of Joyce's *Dubliners*. Unfortunately, economical stories of this sort (where not a word is wasted and much is implied) are often misread, for the simple language and seemingly straightforward narration may relax the reader into overlooking subtleties and ironies meant to darken the story's tone and complicate its tragedy. Furthermore, the subject matter of "He"—coping with the psychological and physical demands of raising a retarded child—is one that causes many readers to sympathize with Mrs. Whipple instead of judging her according to the story's evidence. My objectives in this paper are, first, to indicate how the story should be read and, then, to establish the view that Porter expects the reader to take toward Mrs. Whipple.

"He" is a *tour de force* in using point of view to unveil the hypocrisy of a character. We learn Mrs. Whipple's sentiments in two ways: directly, through quotation, and indirectly, through the restatement of her words by a third-person narrator. The narrator paraphrases accurately, but, in the story's opening paragraphs, qualifies Mrs. Whipple's noble and loving assertions by reminding us that she makes them only when the neighbors are (or might be) listening and by "loading" his descriptions with tags such as "would say," "kept saying," "forever saying so," and "keep on saying it." Thus, we learn immediately that the narrator is ironic. In reality, Mrs. Whipple is vain and self-deluding and often unaware of, or incapable of admitting, her true motives. In order to understand Mrs. Whipple, we must remember that throughout the story her assertions are exaggerated contradictions of her actual feelings.

Porter's focus is on Mrs. Whipple's relationship with her retarded son, and in the opening scenes we discover the conditional nature of that relationship. The narrator mentions that her claims of a monumental love for Him are made only in front of the neighbors. Mrs. Whipple's priorities are further clarified when she explains to her husband the reason for this great love: "It's natural for a mother . . . it's more natural for a mother to be that way. People don't expect so much of fathers, some way" (p. 49). [All references to the story and the single reference to "Maria Concepcion" are from *The Collected Stories of Katherine Anne Porter* (New York: New American Library, 1970) and are cited parenthetically in the text.] In the repetition of the idea of her love as being "natural" and in her concern for what people expect, we note the unnaturalness of her "love." Although she would not admit the fact, even to herself, Mrs. Whipple's relationship with Him is dictated by what others would think, not by motherly love or tenderness.

That is, Mrs. Whipple's public relationship with Him is governed by her anticipation of the neighbors' reactions. For when Mrs. Whipple is alone with Him and does not expect the neighbors to visit, eavesdrop, or spy, her true attitude toward Him becomes apparent, at least to the reader. John E. Hardy claims that the preacher's assurance that He enjoys God's special protection ("The innocent walk with God") has been valuable to Mrs. Whipple as "an excuse for her own neglect and exploitation of Him." However, Mrs. Whipple's treatment of her son in private suggests her intentions go further than neglect and exploitation. When Mrs. Whipple tells her neighbors, "I wouldn't have anything happen to Him for all the world, but it just looks like I can't keep Him out of mischief" (p. 50), we search for the reality behind that seemingly loving, but defensive, assertion. We quickly realize that, unconsciously or subconsciously, she desires His death, provided she cannot be blamed for it.

The evidence is copious. She allows Him to climb peach trees until a neighbor, concerned for His safety, warns her that she shouldn't let Him do that (p. 50). She permits Him to handle the bees in their apiary, for He doesn't mind their stings, until, once again, she becomes fearful of what the neighbors might say (p. 51). She boxes Him on the ears because He got His clothes dirty, unaware of how hard she has hit Him until she notices Him fighting back tears and rubbing His head. Then she gets scared and has to sit down because her knees are trembling (pp. 52–53). She gives her daughter Emly the extra blanket off His bed (p. 50) and provides warm clothes for both her other children, claiming that they cannot afford the same for Him (p. 54). Yet He is the one taken sick in February. The Whipples fret for two days, His condition growing no better, before they finally send for the doctor, who tells them He must be kept warm. Mrs. Whipple is ashamed, for, not being able to stand dirt, she has washed His blanket and they must wait until it dries to put it back on His bed. So the Whipples give Him the blanket off their bed and put His cot by the fire, but again Mrs. Whipple is motivated by her fear of gossip: "They can't say we didn't do everything for Him . . . even to sleeping cold ourselves on His account" (p. 55).

Mrs. Whipple's death wish for Him manifests itself less clearly, but not less significantly, in His encounters with the pig and with the bull. When her older son Adna refuses to take a baby pig away from its mother because "That sow'd rip my insides out all over the pen" (p. 52), Mrs. Whipple pushes Him into the pen, claiming He's not afraid. The mother pig is "a great fighter, worse than a Jersey cow" (p. 52). He comes running back, suckling pig in His arms, the sow "raging at His heels" (p. 52).

Encouraging Him to court danger is not the only way that Mrs. Whipple displays her death wish for Him on this occasion. Hendrick notes that in this scene the description of the pink pig is almost the same as descriptions of Him. Indeed, throughout the story the physical description of Him is reminiscent of a pig: for example, "Rolls of fat covered Him like an overcoat" (p. 50) and "He blubbered and rolled" (p. 56). After He catches the piglet, Mrs. Whipple takes it from Him and, with her face stiff, slices its throat in a stroke. He runs at the sight of the pig's blood, but Mrs. Whipple assures herself that He'll forget and eat plenty just the same. She cannot, however, stop thinking about Him:

> "It's a shame, a shame," she kept saying under her breath, "and Adna with so much brains!"
> She kept on feeling badly about all sorts of things. In the first place it was the man's work to butcher; the sight of the pig scraped pink and naked made her sick. He was too fat and soft and pitiful-looking. It was simply a shame the way things had to happen.
>
> (p. 52)

Mrs. Whipple's stream-of-conscious self-pity underlines how closely she too connects her son to the pig. Reviewing her feelings about the pig, scraped pink and naked, triggers the thought of Him. The link between the butchered pig and Him is thus too obvious to overlook: both make her sick. We may deduce that when she cut the pig's throat she was also thinking of Him, and that this confused lamentation is partly an effort to propitiate her conscience, to prevent it from accusing her of the wish to murder. We recall the similar action of another Porter character with a death wish, Maria Concepcion, who soon after she discovers her husband's infidelity, selects a chicken for the archeologist Givens and "silently, swiftly drew her knife across its throat, twisting the head off with the casual firmness she might use with the top of a beet" (p. 7). Givens is unnerved by Maria's cold-bloodedness, but her resoluteness here is an explicit foreshadowing of her later bloody revenge.

The incident with the bull reinforces the impression that Mrs. Whipple harbors an unconscious death wish for Him. The Whipples borrow a bull for breeding purposes from a neighbor, and once again Mrs.

Whipple excuses Adna and sends Him to perform a dangerous job—bringing the bull back to the Whipples' farm. After He has been gone for some time, however, she begins to worry and goes out to the lane to wait for Him. When she finally sees Him, coming slowly and leading the bull behind Him, she panics:

> Mrs. Whipple was scared sick of bulls; she had heard awful stories about how they followed on quietly enough, and then suddenly pitched on with a bellow and pawed and gored a body to pieces. Any second now that black monster would come down on Him, my God, He'd never have sense enough to run.
>
> She mustn't make a sound nor a move; she mustn't get the bull started.

(p. 55)

Significantly, right after she cautions herself to be still, Mrs. Whipple sees the bull move his head at a fly and "Her voice burst out of her in a shriek, and she screamed at Him to come on, for God's sake" (p. 55). Fear causes Mrs. Whipple to endanger His life. However, her fear is not for her son's safety; rather, she is afraid that an accident would ensure the neighbors' scorn because she had let Him undertake a dangerous task. Running toward the house, she prays, "Lord, don't let anything happen to Him. Lord, you *know* people will say we oughtn't to have sent Him. You *know* they'll say we didn't take care of Him. Oh, get Him home, safe home, safe home, and I'll look out for Him better! Amen" (Porter's emphasis, p. 56).

Psychoanalysts tell us that death wishes are not uncommon to parents, especially to the mother, of a retarded child. Maud Mannoni, a French psychoanalyst who has studied the mother-retarded child relationship, emphasizes the intensity and frequency of the mother's death wish: "The mother-child love relationship will always, in such cases, have an aftertaste of death about it, of death denied, of death disguised usually as sublime love, sometimes as pathological indifference, and occasionally as conscious rejection; but the idea of murder is there, even if the mother is not always conscious of it." Simon Olshansky observes that parents of a simple-minded child have little to look forward to, which leads them to search for a permanent escape: "they will always be burdened by the child's unrelenting demands and unabated dependency. The woes, the trials, the moments of despair will continue until either their own deaths or the child's death. Concern about what will happen to his child after he is dead may be a realistic concern for a parent, or it may be associated with death wishes, either for himself or for his child. Release from his chronic sorrow may be obtainable only through death." Thus, besides selfish reasons for wishing for a child's death, Olshansky's investigation uncovers humanitarian motives.

If we ignore the ironic narrator who dictates viewpoint in Porter's story and attribute Mrs. Whipple's death wishes to her worry over her son's future, we might argue for humanitarian motives and conclude as Harry J. Mooney does:

> In "He," we have the story of a mother whose whole life lies in her feeble-minded son, and whose final tragedy comes to her when she is forced to put him in the county home. Mrs. Whipple is not to be blamed for the fact that her son is a mental defective, but she is altogether committed to Him . . . both because she loves him and because he is absolutely dependent upon her. . . . But the real significance of Mrs. Whipple's life lies in her effort to make a life for her son, little though she can help; otherwise his going off to the county home would be a solution to a pressing problem rather than a grim tragedy in a mother's life.

Mooney's sympathetic interpretation of Mrs. Whipple cannot be accepted—first, because we should not overlook (as Mooney has) the ironic third-person narrator, and second, because Mrs. Whipple is *not* the typical mother of a retarded child. Mooney's belief that Mrs. Whipple loves her son is far from accurate. Indeed, as I have indicated, Mrs. Whipple's attitude toward her son is dictated entirely by her selfish concern for appearances. Furthermore, I would argue that His going to the county home *is* a solution to Mrs. Whipple's pressing problem, and, if so, the story's ending requires a very different response from the reader than the one Mooney proposes. The crux of our understanding of the story lies in determining Mrs. Whipple's motives for sending Him to the county home and in analyzing her feelings in the final scene.

When the doctor advises the Whipples to put Him in an institution, Mrs. Whipple promptly refuses. Her reasons, however, are far from loving ones: she does not want the neighbors saying she sent her sick child off among strangers, and she refuses to depend on charity. But Mr. Whipple maintains that He will be better cared for at the county home and assures his wife that they are not accepting charity when their taxes support the place. Once Mrs. Whipple finds excuses with which to fend off neighbors' gossip, His fate is settled. Almost cheerfully, she states that they'll bring Him home when He's better, although, as Mr. Whipple reminds her, the doctor has diagnosed His condition as untreatable. "Doctors don't know everything," Mrs. Whipple retorts (p. 57), but immediately we see that Mrs. Whipple's optimism is intended to delude herself and others as to her true motives.

Clearly, she does not desire His return. When she begins to make plans for their family, she remarks, ". . . we'll all work together and get on our feet again, and the children will feel they've got a place to come to" (p. 57). In other words, without Him, family life will be normal, and the farm will become profitable. In her exultation she envisions summertime, "with the garden going fine, and new white roller shades up all over the house, and Adna and Emly home, so full of life, all of them happy together. Oh, it could happen, things would ease up on them" (pp. 57–58). Although He has been a real help around the farm, even doing Adna's chores when he left to take a job, Mrs. Whipple associates Him with their hardship. The stigma of having a retarded child is more than the vain Mrs. Whipple can bear. Having at last found a way to get rid of Him, other than by His "accidental" death, she plans to do so.

The final scene of mother and child in the neighbor's wagon is the most difficult to assess because Mrs. Whipple finally *seems* to feel some compunction over her previous cruel treatment of Him. If we can determine that that guilt is a small sign of love or the indication of a change of heart, Mrs. Whipple would gain in complexity and become the tragic figure that Mooney claims she is. We note first that Mrs. Whipple is accompanying Him to the county home because of her concern not for Him but about the neighbors: "The hospital would have sent an ambulance, but Mrs. Whipple couldn't stand to see Him going away looking so sick as all that" (p. 58). Second, she continues her story about her plans for Him when, to the neighbor driving the carryall, she asserts: "Besides, it ain't as if He was going to stay forever. . . . This is only for a little while" (p. 58).

Mrs. Whipple apparently expects an uneventful ride, a quick trip to the county home. But as she sits holding her son in her arms, she is amazed to see big tears rolling out of the corners of His eyes. She instantly believes He is accusing her of something: "Maybe He remembered that time she boxed His ears, maybe He had been scared that day with the bull, maybe He had slept cold and couldn't tell her about it; maybe He knew they were sending Him away for good and all because they were too poor to keep Him. Whatever it was, Mrs. Whipple couldn't bear to think of it . . . there was nothing she could do to make up to Him for His life" (p. 58). Mrs. Whipple has not admitted her death wishes, but she has a complete inventory of them running through her mind. And she has given herself away, contradicting in this more lucid, private moment her previous claim that His institutionalization is only temporary (although even privately she rationalizes that decision with the economic excuse). But, primarily, she refuses to think about Him or to try to understand His feelings. As Hardy notes: "She is herself so incapable of genuine charity, of love, that she cannot recognize even the possibility that His weeping is an expression of love for her—an appeal, simply, that He not be turned out of the family, rather than a reproach for what He has suffered there."

The final scene, then, not only reaffirms Mrs. Whipple's callousness, but also confirms His sensitive nature, which previously Porter has only hinted at. We recall, for instance, that He gasped and ran at the sight of blood when Mrs. Whipple sliced the suckling pig's throat. Mrs. Whipple dismissed His reaction, claiming that He would "forget and eat plenty, just the same" (p. 52). However, during the Sunday meal, He would not enter the dining room where the prepared pig was being carved. Mrs. Whipple attributed His refusal to timidity, but knowing her habit of rationalization, we might more plausibly argue that His reluctance arises from His memory of the butchering of the pig. At one point in the story Mrs. Whipple chastises her husband for calling Him senseless. Pretending to understand Him, she maintains, "He sees a lot that goes on, He listens to things all the time" (p. 51). Ironically, Mrs. Whipple is right. For although the Whipples are careful not to discuss their plans for His institutionalization in front of Him, He seems to know He is being sent away. His dumbness becomes that much more painful to the reader, for He cannot protest or prevent His fate.

As in Greek tragedy where blindness is an indication of "sight," in Porter's story dumbness becomes a sign of awareness. His understanding coupled with His dependency—and contrasted to Mrs. Whipple's deception and selfishness—makes Mrs. Whipple's victimization of Him even more appalling. As Mrs. Whipple observes, He does anything she tells Him to do (p. 51). Yet she cannot accept Him for what He is, nor can she love Him. Her final thought is "what a mortal pity He was ever born" (p. 58), a feeling the neighbors voiced behind her back and the death wish she can finally admit—now that He will no longer cause her misery. As far as she is concerned, He is dead.

Having identified Mrs. Whipple's motives throughout the story and having understood the total lack of love she feels for her son, we can hardly feel compassion for her, as many critics do, at the story's end. In fact, Emmons' hope that Mrs. Whipple's "desire for order and a better life might find a way to help luck along" now seems terribly ironic; Mooney's conclusion that "the real significance of Mrs. Whipple's life lies in her effort to make a life for her son" is simply a misreading. Even Hardy's suggestion that Mrs. Whipple's incapacity is "the common incapacity of mankind, the curse of our intelligent being" cannot be accepted; for Porter, with her use of the ironic third-person narrator, does not let us condone that incapacity or the woman who manifests it and tries to pretend otherwise. Mrs. Whipple's hatred of Him, derived from the loss of comfort and prestige that she believes her retarded son has caused her, is despicable, no matter how universal her feeling of injustice might be.

In charting the psychology of the relationship between a mother and her retarded son, Porter actually anticipated by twenty years any extensive efforts of psychoanalysts to examine the same territory. However, "He" should not be viewed as a literary precursor to a scientific enterprise. Porter's purpose is not to depict the psychological and emotional problems that the ordinary mother of a retarded child might face. Instead she is concerned, as she is in many other stories, with self-deception, vanity, and hypocrisy. In "He" Porter shows us not a weak but well-meaning mother of a retarded child, but rather one whose pride and hypocrisy make her a moral monster. To be swayed by Mrs. Whipple's self-serving rationalizations is to miss the point of the story.

JANE KRAUSE DeMOUY

Face to Face: "Old Mortality"

"Old Mortality" completes the story of Miranda's role models. As Jane Flanders has noted, Miranda's Aunt Amy and her Cousin Eva, who dominate the story, have equal, if different, reasons for repudiating the Old Order. Their experiences demonstrate that to be a legendary beauty like Amy in such a society one must sacrifice freedom, and even life. To be independent, a bluestocking, and a suffragist like Eva is to become ossified in bitterness. Part of the point of the story is that everybody in the family has long since decided what to think about Amy and Eva. The only person who has not is the one still capable of learning something about them: Miranda. Behind the history of these women is the curious, quizzical figure of Miranda, sifting and balancing, from the vantage point of adulthood, what she knew when she was eight, then ten, and finally eighteen. It is not Amy's life but Miranda's heritage that one learns about in the three segments of time which end with Miranda's promise to herself to find her own truth, made "in her hopefulness, her ignorance." Those last two words are the judgment of the older narrator on eighteen-year-old Miranda's limited view, just as they are the reader's clue that "Old Mortality" is a fiction of memory in a double sense: it is the memory of her forebears, but it is also Miranda's memory of what she has been and, therefore, what she has become.

In Part I of the story, Miranda is portrayed as easily seduced by romantic illusion. It is her practical-minded sister, Maria, who disabuses her of her notions. Intent on knowing the truth, even at an early age, Miranda is hampered by her childish credulousness. As an eight-year-old, she is most susceptible to every sentiment and every bit of romantic

From *Katherine Anne Porter's Women*. Copyright © 1983 by University of Texas Press.

claptrap that her society is capable of. She listens to the adults around her, consuming everything they say. At the same time, however, she always wonders what they mean, since her interpretation of family events is very much at odds with the interpretation the family places on them. When, for instance, Miranda's father announces that "There were never any fat women in the family, thank God," Miranda thinks immediately of Great-Aunt Eliza's huge frame and Great-Aunt Keziah, who weighs 220 pounds. Later she will be old enough to recognize that

> something seemed to happen to their father's memory when he thought of the girls he had known in the family of his youth, and he declared steadfastly they had all been, in every generation without exception, as slim as reeds and graceful as sylphs.

In truth, something seems to happen to the memory of all the members of this society when they think of their past: "their hearts and imaginations were captivated by their past," which is far more significant to them than the everyday world of the present. The Grandmother, who sits all day making memory quilts with Nannie, feels "twice a year compelled in her blood" to sit by her old trunks "crying gently and easily" over faded finery, pictures, and mementoes. The elderly relative who heard Rubinstein play frequently in the past finds Paderewski lacking in the present. However, it is not just the past but emotion and sentiment that captivate the whole family, and the story of Gabriel's unrequited love for Amy is the family's favorite—and collective—legend.

What Porter says but does not stress is that this family is Southern. Not only do they revere their past, they aggrandize it in a manner that suggests Twain was right when he accused Walter Scott's medieval romances of starting the Civil War. Miranda looks at pictures of the young men "in their high buttoned coats, their puffy neckties, their waxed mustaches, their waving thick hair combed carefully over their foreheads" and thinks no one could have taken them seriously. However, these same young men are romanticized into chivalric heroes whose nobility of purpose defines the whole race. Furthermore, while their eyes and ears tell them that Cousin Molly Parrington's charm is aggressive, bold, and sometimes even cruel or shocking, their imaginations assure them that their women are unequaled not only in their beauty and desirability, but in their purity, gentility, and sensibility. They are the fair virgins of a society whose virtue they both embody and inspire. In actuality, Amy's circumstances combine the poetry and tragedy Miranda's family love with their personal history; their pleasure in Amy's story is like the eight-year-old Miranda's pleasure in thinking what it would be like "to have the assassination of Lincoln in the family."

Similar in structure to "The Old Order," "Old Mortality" is a pastiche of memories, details, and emotions, "floating ends of narrative" which Maria and Miranda patch together as well as they can, the "fragments of tales that were like bits of poetry or music. . . ." And like the memories of the Old Order, they have been "packed away and forgotten for a great many years." It is ostensibly Amy's story, told from a number of points of view, but all is sifted through Miranda's perception. In actuality, the chronology of the story belongs to Miranda, and the tale depends primarily on what she will do with the legend of Amy and the bitter reality of Cousin Eva.

If "The Old Order" is a catalogue of the "giants" of Miranda's childhood who taught her what a woman might be, "Old Morality" is the story of Miranda's confrontation with the most formidable archetype her society can offer: the Southern belle, a nineteenth-century American manifestation of the virgin love goddess.

Obviously, Amy was once a person who has now become a legend; she was "beautiful, much loved, unhappy, and she . . . died young." The mystery in her behavior encourages others to speculate aloud about her and the meaning of her actions. Enigmatic, devilish, magnetic to men, she has also been capricious, toying with Gabriel's affection, agreeing to marry two other men, and then subsequently breaking those engagements without reason. She has been the cause of a near duel and her brother Harry's flight to Mexico; and yet she never offers an explanation of the affair. Finally, after dismissing Gabriel summarily, she whimsically agrees to marry him when he is disinherited. Her family says good-bye to her after her wedding, and six weeks later she is dead, perhaps by suicide.

A more romantic and tragic combination of circumstances is not to be imagined, conjuring as they do the likes of Juliet, Madame Bovary, and Anna Karenina. Then too, Amy is a dark lady—not only Shakespeare's, but Hawthorne's, and certainly Poe's—with more sensuousness and dangerous allure than virginity would ordinarily allow.

Amy's physical beauty supposedly corresponds in every detail to her family's standard of female perfection:

> First, a beauty must be tall; whatever color the eyes, the hair must be dark, the darker the better; the skin must be pale and smooth. Lightness and swiftness of movement were important points. A beauty must be a good dancer, superb on horseback, with a serene manner, an amiable gaiety tempered with dignity at all hours. Beautiful teeth and hands, of course, and over and above all this, some mysterious crown of enchantment that attracted and held the heart.

But it is interesting that Miranda, studying the old-fashioned portrait of Amy with her cropped hair and "reckless smile," is left wondering what was so enticing about this compelling girl, about whom everything and nothing was known. The obvious implication is that Amy was in reality a young woman whose graces and physical charms have been exaggerated by the family, who take more pleasure in the reflected glory they receive from their relationship to this angelic mystery than they do in the accuracy of their descriptions. There is undoubtedly some of that, but there is also the persistent fact that Amy really was a charmer, with at least two other suitors who wanted to marry her. There is something more to Amy's dark beauty than an appealing prettiness. A less romantic generation would reject the term "crown of enchantment" and call it sex appeal, but it is not quite the simple matter Cousin Eva makes it, either, when she describes Victorian mating rituals as "just sex." Amy's allure is rather a complex combination of sublimated sexual energy, real allure, and personal restraint.

Like Laura in "Flowering Judas," Amy appears to be a very distinct personality who has made her choices and insists on self-determination despite the efforts of others to influence her. In actuality, however, she is, like Laura, a very ambivalent personality confronted by a now familiar dichotomy: the choice between being a sexual coquette or marrying to become a mother. The lessons of her society for young unmarried females are contained not only in their code of female beauty, but in the more concrete example of the behavior of Miranda's father toward his daughters:

> [He] held his daughters on his knee if they were prettily dressed and well-behaved, and pushed them away if they had not freshly combed hair and nicely scrubbed fingernails. "Go away, you're disgusting," he would say.

Amy has long since assimilated these lessons and mastered them; in fact, if her family is to be believed, she has raised coquetry to a high art, learning not only to display her beauty, but to flaunt her sexuality while forbidding intimacy. While she probably has little understanding of sex as a physical act, she intuitively recognizes that her physical attributes attract men and that she can entice with impunity, even irresponsibility, as long as she retains her virginity. While her family acts as if she has no control over the way men respond to her, Amy herself understands and relishes the power this gives her.

Holding the prize in abeyance as long as possible allows Amy a fleeting personal autonomy she doesn't want to relinquish. She insists that she doesn't want to marry anybody, saying she prefers to be a "nice old maid like Eva Parrington." Her Uncle Bill, referring to Eva's political activity, casually puts a finger on the sexual nature of the courtship game: "When women haven't anything else, they'll take a vote for consolation. A pretty thin bed-fellow." Significantly, Amy responds: "What I really need is a good dancing partner to guide me through life," which is perhaps a wish for a strong man who will make less fearsome her plunge into sexual experience. This meaning is well illustrated by the Mardi Gras party and the "scandal" which ensues after Amy's tryst there with a former fiancé.

A time of revelry and chaos preceding the mourning and fasting of Lent, Mardi Gras sets the tone for Amy's brush with sexual and social disaster. Her costume for the fancy-dress ball is a carefully copied shepherdess outfit, which underscores the *carpe diem* atmosphere, complete with low-cut bodice, short skirts which reveal her ankles, and rouge on her cheeks. Amy's father throws a fit and declares her outfit "bawdy," while, significantly, her mother sees "nothing wrong with it" and chides her husband for using "such language before innocent young girls." Having been a belle herself, Amy's mother recognizes that her daughter's sex appeal is one of the few cards she has to play in the courtship game. Gabriel, attired to please Amy, looks like the sentimental fop he is in a blue satin shepherd's costume and curled beribboned wig. He is no match, much less a guide, for Amy's overt sexuality, and as the other young men swarm to her like flies to a honey pot, Gabriel is hardly able to dance with her at all.

In stark contrast to Gabriel, Raymond, a former fiancé of Amy's, arrives late and alone, with all the air of a nocturnal lover come in over his lady's balcony. He appears as the daring pirate Jean Lafitte and boldly takes Amy's attention from the others. After a sojourn with Raymond on the gallery, she waltzes by "with a young man in a Devil costume, including ill-fitting scarlet cloven hoofs," a costume which stresses Amy's attraction to sin, passion, and a satyr-inspired sex, and the ultimate irony of her own arcadian attire.

The foils to Amy's particular brand of womanliness are only subtly characterized. Mariana, Harry's bride-to-be and eventually the mother of Miranda projects none of Amy's sauciness, despite the fact that she wears Mexican dress, from a country where the women are said to be spitfires. Maria and Miranda remember a picture of their mother: "her lovely face without a trace of coquetry looking gravely out from under a tremendous fall of lace from the peak of the comb, a rose tucked firmly over her ear." It is Mariana who should be wearing the simple shepherdess costume and Amy who should portray the sultry Mexican. However, part of Amy's appeal lies in the fact that although she aggressively displays her sexuality, she puts a demure mask over it; she has some of the same tantalizing air as a Lolita: a naïf with a smoldering appetite.

She is hardly "sweet and gay and decorous" as her second foil—her own mother—was when she was courted. Her mother, who has found identity in nurturing, tries to tell Amy "that marriage and children would cure her of everything." But offspring are not the end she looks for; neither is marriage itself or even a particular man. Amy's disguised sexual anxiety and wish for personal autonomy are not desires she can name herself. She knows only an intense longing and a nagging anticipation of death which implies both the futility of her desires within her social structure ("Mammy, I'm not long for this world") and the physical de-struction she anticipates. A woman born to a society which saw her father as her protector until a husband took over that necessary role, Amy is protected to a degree which destroys personal privacy, to say nothing of individuality or initiative. The fact that she cannot momentarily leave her social group in the company of a man without stirring up scandal, even to the outer reaches of her community, is proof of her confinement.

It is significant, too, that although Amy curries the favor of her brothers and undoubtedly practices feminine wiles on her suitors, "she would not listen to her father, nor to Gabriel," the two men most intent on ruling her in this life. Her response is unequivocal. She ignores her father's demands that she wear a more modest costume to the Mardi Gras ball, and when Gabriel praises her long hair, she cuts it short both to assert her independence of his image of her and to divest herself of a demure femininity that seems oppressive to her. Significantly, when Gabriel accuses her of having been kissed by Raymond, she insists that he was merely complimenting her on her hair. Her pleasure in a compliment like that is, ironically, a greater infidelity to Gabriel than a stolen kiss—very likely an impulsive gesture.

Gabriel, in his doglike devotion, is an encumbrance to Amy—and not only because his courtship represents a serious threat to her virginity. Since she cannot be a belle without the attentions of a swain, however, her victimizer becomes a victim of the sentimental society which glamor-izes these roles. While her beauty is legendary, in the best tradition of courtly love, beauty must be praised in song and service to be considered noteworthy. Amy's legend is at least partly dependent on the fervor of Gabriel's courtship: the presents, flowers, telegrams, and defense of her honor are all the concrete proof of her desirability. In truth, Gabriel plays the Southern knight so well that he continues the role years after Amy's death, composing sentimental poetry to her memory and supervising the carving of her tombstone even after he has taken a new wife.

For her part, Amy cultivates her dramatic image, calling herself "the heroine of this novel." She chooses to marry Gabriel only after he is disinherited, and then tells him they must be wed before Mardi Gras because after Lent "it may be too late." For her wedding day she disdains the colorlessness and the connotations of white satin; she does not wish to look pale, angelic, bridelike, or pure, and chooses instead an individualistic gown of silver gray silk. The wintry gray of her costume is unbroken except for a "dark red breast of feathers" on her gray velvet hat, which suggests the mortal wound which is her illness, and her marriage, and her womanhood—and which she herself seems to intend: "I shall wear mourning if I like," she tells her mother, "it is *my* funeral, you know."

Her one letter home illustrates that she has not changed, despite her statement that she is now "a staid old married woman." On the contrary, she goes to the races daily and delights in the successes of their horses. She wants to take to the streets during Mardi Gras because she is tired of "watching the show from a balcony." Like Laura, she covets excitement. Gabriel will be her escort in the frenzied streets of the carnival if she can convince him to descend, but he "says it isn't safe." Remembering her wish for a good dancing partner to guide her through life, one cannot help but note this symbolic allusion to Gabriel's insufficiency as a husband. He has always lacked boldness and masculinity in Amy's eyes, and his ineffectual behavior at the first Mardi Gras ball as well as his reluctance to become part of the new chaos on his honeymoon suggest he is at least a reluctant or an inept lover, and very possibly an intimidated one. Amy's reiterated insistence that Gabriel is "dull" makes it clear that he is no real threat to her virginity. But a man like Raymond is, not only because he is more aggressive than Gabriel, but because Amy finds him sexually exciting. Fearing the experience of sex itself and the potential rowdiness of her own sexuality, Amy has broken her engagement to Raymond, ultimately choosing a safer Gabriel.

Why, then, does she choose to marry at all? It may be that, anticipating her death, she leaps into chaos (or certainly a world of excitement, if not frenzy); she chooses the only opportunity she has to marry quickly and experience the worldly pleasure of sex symbolized by New Orleans with its races, the parades and balls of Mardi Gras, and the "dashing" dress she chooses to wear to the Proteus Ball. It could be also that in marrying Gabriel she does not relinquish her virginity at all, since he will do anything to please her, and this leaves her psychologically free to flirt and act the part of the unmarried belle in her new gown. A third and more complicated possibility is that the confinement and restriction of her training has effected a psychology in her which values restraint more than any other physical reality. Thus even if she consummates her marriage to Gabriel, her psychic detachment from intercourse allows her to think of herself as inviolate because she has not been excited by it. Physically she may not be a virgin, but emotionally and psychologically she is intact. Thus her marriage to Gabriel would be a real rejection of sexual participation and experience, and she could continue her pattern of sexual display and restraint. True to her anticipation, six weeks after her wedding—exactly the length of Lent, which, ironically, ends in the celebration of resurrected life—Amy is dead of a combination of consumption and medicinal overdose.

The whole issue of Amy's illness and death is a compelling and complex subject. Her death and its romantic significance to the family is well established before Amy's illness is even mentioned, and her problem is never named in specific terms. Her mother assures her that all the women of their family suffered delicacy and all survived; she adds that "young girls found a hundred ways to deny they wished to be married. . . ." The conjunction of these two conditions suggests first that this delicacy is a fear of the sexual reality of marriage, for that is the only illness that can be cured by marriage and children:

> I tried to tell her once more . . . that marriage and children would cure her of everything. . . . "Why when I was your age no one expected me to live a year. It was called greensickness, and everybody knew there was only one cure."

Only as a virgin is she "green," a sexual novice. After marriage and birth, a woman is initiated into sexual mysteries and is thereby "cured" of her illness—that is, her fears. Of course, Amy's malady is not so readily assuaged. She has tuberculosis, a debilitating, and, in Amy's day, often fatal disease. Metaphorically, however, her consumption, which forces her to go to bed and to expel blood from her body, suggests menstruation—which in the past has been called "the curse" by many women. Conversely, of course, "curse" describes consumption. Tuberculosis was also thought to enhance the beauty of its victim, since under its influence the eyes sparkled with fever and spots of color appeared in the cheeks, just as menstruation is a sign of physical maturity, which makes a female more sexually appealing. Thus, symbolically, Amy's illness must represent her womanhood, a biological and social handicap to a free spirit.

Each of the three attacks she experiences during the last year of her life occurs after some breach of feminine restraint on her part. The first serious illness is brought on by her three-day ride to the Mexican border; the second occurs after she stays up all night dancing three times in one week; and the third results from her round of races and Mardi Gras parties in New Orleans. It is blood that keeps her in bounds, and when she steps beyond the bounds of her feminine role, she pays in blood. Should she marry and bear children, she will pay in blood anyway. She is the ultimate portrait of a woman in suspension. It is supremely ironic that the only outspoken "feminist" in the family, Eva, who crusades for female suffrage, is Amy's harshest critic, with no sympathy for Amy, who is suffocating in her confined role.

It is Eva who in her bitter jealousy can only see Amy as a "bad, wild girl" who was *"too free"* and who was "sex-ridden" and "festering." She provides a warped kind of balance to the romantic image of Amy, and she focuses attention on Amy's enigmatic death. Eva implies that Amy was pregnant by another man when she married Gabriel and that she killed herself "to escape some disgrace. . . ." In her rage to hang infamy on Amy's memory, Eva ignores the obvious facts that, once Amy had a husband, she could bear a child without "disgrace" or "exposure" and that Amy was one who sought the public eye rather than avoided it. Eva is projecting her own feelings, perhaps, but she has no understanding of Amy as a person and reacts only to what Amy represents.

Amy would not commit suicide to avoid scandal; but would she commit suicide to fulfill an image she has of herself? It is both possible and characteristic that, recognizing the limited options she has, she chooses a last whirl around the dance floor, a last moment of gaiety and glory and then rings down the curtain on her own role. Unable to choose how she will live, she chooses instead the way she will die. Instead of fading into a ragged oblivion, she dramatically snuffs out her life (whether by accident or design) so that her beauty and mystery are etched in the memory: "She ran into the gray cold . . . and called out 'Good-by, good-by!' . . . And none of us ever saw her alive again."

It is possible that Amy inadvertently took an overdose of medication, although she doesn't appear to have ever done anything else inadvertently. Her consistently fatalistic outlook suggests she knows she will die young. It is also possible that she is pregnant by her husband and that, recognizing that she can no longer retain her independence, she kills herself in a direct refusal to share her life or her identity with a child. Does she intuit or intend her death? Ultimately it doesn't really matter— her "prophetic" remarks may even be the interpolation of the family mythmakers. What does matter, to Miranda especially, is that her end is death. Although she is beautiful, much loved, sought after, and greatly desired—although she marries as she should—she still dies young. Although she marries with detachment and with no unseemly passion in it, she is still struck down. As to the cause, she is at least weakened by her disease, in both its physical and its symbolic sense. She is handicapped by a weakened constitution and by a sexuality she cannot come to terms with; perhaps the point is not so much that these conditions cause her death but that in the face of them she cannot live.

Ordinarily, a Porter story would end here with a death of a kind visited on a woman ill equipped to get out of its way. But the story is as much Miranda's as it is Amy's, and the second and third parts bring her back into focus, partly by extending the imagery of Amy's experience to Miranda and Maria. Like Amy, they feel "hedged and confined" by a conventional life in their boarding school. Like her, they suffer a constant surveillance by their chaperones, the nuns, and find their lives incredibly "dull" except for Saturday afternoon trips to the races, where excitement reigns.

The symbolic value of the horses to which this family is devoted is one of the significant links between Parts I and II and between Amy and Miranda. Amy loves to ride and uses horses as a vehicle for excitement and adventure. The races in New Orleans relieve her boredom and furnish her delight when one of their horses wins. More important, however, the way family members use their horses is indicative of their stature as human beings. The family has always enjoyed owning and racing horses, but among gentlemen this is a pursuit of pleasure, not a livelihood. The first inkling Miranda has that Gabriel is less than his legend lies in the episode in which he and his grandfather quarrel over his racehorses. His grandfather fears he will be a wastrel who will use his horses to make a living, and his fear is prophetic; it foreshadows Gabriel's decline and Miranda's disillusionment in Part II. However, these details are only transitions to the large meaning of "Old Mortality."

In Part II, romance opens outward and the real issues of the whole story begin to take shape. Maria and Miranda, now fourteen and ten, are separated from their family circle in a convent school in New Orleans. Their romantic, penny-dreadful image of themselves does not mask the fact that they are about to experience an initiation. They are already in the midst of the first classic stage of rites of passage: separation from their communal circle. They allude to an actual initiation ceremony, the taking of the veil; the familiar image of burial, with an expected resurrection and rebirth, is suggested by the word "immured," which the girls delight in applying to themselves. In the course of events, Miranda will further experience the second stage of initiation: isolation.

As a small girl given to illusion, Miranda has aspired to be "a tall, cream-colored brunette, like cousin Isabel. . . ." But by the age of ten, she has decided to become a jockey instead. Incongruous and humorous as it is, her choice illustrates that Miranda has already assimilated the lessons of the Old Order and the conflict that will be her adult legacy: she moves from a traditionally feminine idol to a masculine hero and eschews beauty for independence and excitement. The same division is obvious when she rejects Spanish-style riding for the jockey's bounce.

Part II focuses on a Saturday afternoon when the girls have been taken to the races by their father to watch Uncle Gabriel's horse, Miss Lucy, run. Despite bad odds, the horse wins, and Miranda has her first encounter with the real Uncle Gabriel and the reality of a horse race. Uncle Gabriel disheartens the girls immediately with his "coarse" language and loud voice, and he soon proves to be a drunkard. He abuses himself and his horses as well, for he hasn't enough pride to earn a living by some occupation. He depends on his horses for survival, and what once was a pleasure is now desperate necessity. The ignominiousness of this situation comes home to Miranda when she sees Miss Lucy as the family members descend to the winner's circle:

> Miss Lucy was bleeding at the nose, two thick red rivulets were stiffening her tender mouth and chin, the round velvet chin that Miranda thought the nicest kind of chin in the world. Her eyes were wild and her knees were trembling, and she snored when she drew her breath.

Miranda stares with "her heart clinched tight. . . ." She feels "instantly and completely . . . her heart reject that victory . . ."; hating what she sees, she feels ashamed for screaming for joy when the horse came in a winner. This is the same image we have of Miranda in the forest beside her brother and the dead rabbit, saying "Oh, I want to *see*" and, seeing, rejecting the victory. Miranda is once again repelled by the reality of the horse's blood and suffering, and in rejecting that reality, she effectively isolates herself from her uncle, father, and sister. She wants nothing else to do with the painful victory of a horse that has won heroically for a heavy man with sour breath and rumpled clothing.

Uncle Gabriel effectively destroys the rest of the afternoon for them by leading them home through a seamy neighborhood to meet his ungracious second wife, who obviously can't stand the sight of Amy's relatives and won't forbear to quarrel with her husband in front of them. The whole affair is a descent into Gabriel's particular circle of hell; he lives in a run-down hotel located, ironically, in a section of town called Elysian Fields. It is indeed a land of the dead, but instead of the warmth and peace connoted by the name, an icy tension pervades this place, and Miranda and Maria are grateful to escape. Encompassing both the image of Amy on the one hand and the successful jockey on the other, Gabriel's sleaziness taints Miranda's imagination in two directions at once. Surely the image of Amy herself must waver a bit now that Miranda has seen exposed the clay feet of Amy's hero.

In Part III, Miranda, now eighteen and married herself, is return-ing home for Uncle Gabriel's funeral when she meets her cousin Eva Parrington, who has the same destination. Their conversation is a re-minder that the more things change, the more they remain the same. Miranda still has daredevil aspirations, and Eva still bitterly nurses old wounds inflicted by the family in her youth. The ugly relative is clearly meant to balance the beautiful one, and Eva is Amy's opposite in every way. Not only does she offer a personal contrast to Amy's life and style; she also gives Miranda her own nasty version of Amy's story; but her obvious jealousy and her mercenary spirit discredit her. We wind up discovering more about Eva than we do about Amy. While Amy married for her own puzzling motives, Eva, given the chance, would have done worse: she would have married for money. She finally ends her tirade by condemning Amy and her "rivals" for playing the courting game: "It was just sex . . .; their minds dwelt on nothing else . . . , so they simply festered inside—they festered—." She succeeds primarily in describing herself; when Miranda tries to assert that Eva is too extreme by suggesting that her mother was not like that, Eva retorts easily and automatically, "Your mother was a saint," and dismisses the subject.

In view of the initiation pattern established in Part II, one might expect Part III to bring about Miranda's reintegration with her family circle. She does seem hesitantly aware that she might become like Eva, and admires the courage and heroism of her crusade for women's rights. She cringes, however, at the prospect of looking so "withered and tired . . . so *old*" and finally is completely repelled by Eva's invective:

> "Beauty goes, character stays" . . . It was a dreary prospect; why was a strong character so deforming? Miranda felt she truly wanted to be strong, but how could she face it, seeing what it did to one?

At this point Miranda clearly sees a dichotomy between beauty and character. It is not only an axiom from her childhood but a division she has absorbed from her experience among her family. Even more important, Miranda has proved herself attractive enough to "catch a husband," but her own marriage was an impetuous elopement that has given her no true home. When she mentions it to Eva, her thoughts are completely negative:

> It seemed very unreal even as she said it, and seemed to have nothing at all to do with the future; . . . the only feeling she could rouse in herself about it was an immense weariness as if it were an illness that she might one day hope to recover from.

It will not take her life as it has Amy's, but then Miranda will not exactly recover from it, either. So Miranda is caught between the negative image of one alternative and her own dissatisfying experience of the second.

As children do, Miranda hopes her father will make it right by welcoming her home, but she is beyond that and he rejects her. She realizes that "It is I who have no place" and feels "her blood [rebel] against the ties of blood," those "bonds that smothered her in love and hatred." She resolves characteristically that she will stay in no place and with no person that might forbid her making "her own discoveries." Ultimately she promises herself that, barring all else, she will know the truth about her own experiences. Unfortunately, the truth she has yet to know will not make her free, either.

Chronology

<table>
<tr><td>1890</td><td>Born May 15 in Indian Creek, Texas, to Mary Alice Jones Porter and Harrison Porter.</td></tr>
<tr><td>1892</td><td>Her mother dies. The family moves to Kyle, Texas, where she is cared for by her grandmother, Catherine Anne Porter, a devout Methodist.</td></tr>
<tr><td>1901</td><td>Her grandmother dies.</td></tr>
<tr><td>1901–05</td><td>Lives with father and various relatives in Texas. Spends a year on farm of father's cousin Ellen Skaggs Thompson in Buda, the setting for the short novel, Noon Wine. Has one year of formal schooling in The Thomas School in San Antonio, a nonsectarian school with strong Methodist leanings, where she studies drama, singing and music.</td></tr>
<tr><td>1906–14</td><td>Elopes with John Henry Koontz, a clerk in the Southern Pacific Railway Company and of wealthy Catholic background. Marries him in a civil ceremony at the age of sixteen. Lives with him in several places for seven years, eventually divorced in 1915. During this time, converts to Catholicism.</td></tr>
<tr><td>1914</td><td>Works in Chicago for movies and newspapers for six months. Goes on Lyceum Circuit performing songs and poems.</td></tr>
<tr><td>1917</td><td>Works for a Fort Worth, Texas, newspaper.</td></tr>
<tr><td>1918–19</td><td>Works in Denver for Rocky Mountain News. May have experienced love affair eventually commemorated in "Pale Horse, Pale Rider." Nearly dies of influenza, which kills (possible) lover and which she feels divides her life. Beloved niece dies, further alienating her—she does not see her family again for fifteen years.</td></tr>
<tr><td>1920</td><td>Resides in New York City, supporting herself in various jobs, among them, ghostwriting, studio publicity and composing ballets for Diaghilev.</td></tr>
<tr><td>1920–22</td><td>Frequently in Mexico, studying Mexican art, and beginning to write her own stories.</td></tr>
<tr><td>1922</td><td>First story she admits authorship of, "María Concepción," published.</td></tr>
<tr><td>1926</td><td>Marries and divorces, Ernest Stock.</td></tr>
</table>

1929 "The Jilting of Granny Weatherall."

1930 *Flowering Judas.*

1931 Returns to Mexico. Friendship and then violent disputes with Hart Crane. Sails from Mexico to Europe on Guggenheim Fellowship, making the voyage the basis for *Ship of Fools* later.

1933 Marriage with Eugene Pressley.

1935 Second, expanded edition of *Flowering Judas.*

1936 Renews personal ties with family. Begins story, "Promised Land," which after 25 years becomes *Ship of Fools.*

1938 Divorces Pressley, marries Albert Erskine (divorced in 1942).

1939 *Pale Horse, Pale Rider.*

1944 *The Leaning Tower and Other Stories.*

1952 *The Days Before* (book of essays).

1955 Changes publishers. Settles down seriously to work on *Ship of Fools.*

1962 *Ship of Fools.*

1965 *Collected Stories,* which wins both the National Book Award and the Pulitzer Prize.

1970 *Collected Essays.*

1977 *The Never-Ending Wrong* (on Sacco-Vanzetti case).

1980 Dies on September 18 at Silver Spring, Maryland.

Contributors

HAROLD BLOOM, Sterling Professor of the Humanities at Yale University, is the author of *The Anxiety of Influence, Poetry and Repression* and many other volumes of literary criticism. His forthcoming study, *Freud: Transference and Authority*, attempts a full-scale reading of all of Freud's major writings. He is the general editor of *The Chelsea House Library of Literary Criticism*.

ROBERT PENN WARREN, our most eminent living man of letters, is best known for his novels, including *All the King's Men* and *World Enough and Time*, and for his poetry, of which the latest collection is *New and Selected Poems: 1923–1985*.

ROBERT B. HEILMAN is Professor Emeritus of English at the University of Washington in Seattle. He is the author of many studies on modern literature and on Shakespeare.

HOWARD MOSS is Poetry Editor of *The New Yorker*. His books include *Selected Poems* and *The Magic Lantern of Marcel Proust*.

EUDORA WELTY is one of our greatest living writers of short stories and novels. Her books include *Delta Wedding* and *The Golden Apples*, and her most recent, *One Writer's Beginnings*.

M. M. LIBERMAN is Professor of English at Grinnell College. His books include *A Preface to Literary Analysis, The Practice of Criticism* and *A Modern Lexicon of Literary Terms*.

CONSTANCE ROOKE is Assistant Professor of English at the University of Victoria, in Canada. Her articles and short stories have appeared in *Southern Review, English Studies in Canada, Fiction International* and *Studies in Short Fiction*, among others.

BRUCE WALLIS is Associate Professor of English at the University of Victoria, in Canada. His articles have appeared in *Studies in Short Fiction, The University of Toronto Quarterly* and others. He has also published a book, *Byron: The Critical Voice*.

JOAN GIVNER is Katherine Anne Porter's biographer and Professor of American

Literature at the University of Regina, in Canada. Several of her articles on Porter have appeared in the *Southwest Review*.

THOMAS F. WALSH is Professor of English at Georgetown University. He has published articles on Porter, Poe, Hawthorne, Howells and Flannery O'Connor in such journals as *Modern Language Notes*, *Modern Language Quarterly*, *Modern Language Journal* and the *Georgia Review*.

JOANN P. COBB is Professor of English at Parks College, Cahokia, Ill.

BRUCE W. JORGENSEN has written poetry, fiction and reviews as well as critical articles. He is Assistant Professor of English at Brigham Young University in Utah.

DEBRA A. MODDELMOG is Professor at Penn State University. She writes on Faulkner and Porter.

JANE KRAUSE DeMOUY lives near Chevy Chase, Maryland.

Bibliography

Baumgartner, Paul R. *Katherine Anne Porter*. New York: American Authors and Critics Series, 1969.

Curley, Daniel. "Treasure in 'The Grave'." *Modern Fiction Studies* 9: 377–84.

DeMouy, Jane Krause. *Katherine Anne Porter's Women*. Austin: University of Texas Press, 1983.

Flanders, Jane. "Katherine Anne Porter's Feminist Criticism: Book Reviews From the 1920's." *Frontiers: A Journal of Women's Studies* 2, vol. 4 (1979): 44–48.

Gardiner, Judith Kegan. " 'The Grave,' 'On Not Shooting Sitting Birds,' and the Female Esthetic." *Studies in Short Fiction* 4, vol. 20 (1983): 265–71.

Givner, Joan. *Katherine Anne Porter: A Life*. New York: Simon and Schuster, 1982.

Gottfried, Leon. "Death's Other Kingdom: Dantesque and Theological Symbolism in 'Flowering Judas'." *PMLA* 84 (1969): 112–24.

Gretlund, Jan Nordby. "Katherine Anne Porter and the South: A Corrective." *The Mississippi Quarterly: The Journal of Southern Culture* 4, vol. 34 (1981): 435–45.

Hafley, James. " 'María Concepción': Life Among the Ruins." *Four Quarters* 12 (November, 1962): 11–17.

Hardy, John Edward. *Katherine Anne Porter*. New York: Frederick Ungar, 1973.

Hartley, Lodwick. "Dark Voyagers: A Study of Katherine Anne Porter's *Ship of Fools*." *University Review* 30 (1963): 83–94.

Hartley, Lodwick and Core, George, eds. *Katherine Anne Porter: A Critical Symposium*. Athens, Georgia: The University of Georgia Press, 1969.

Hendrick, George. *Katherine Anne Porter*. New York: Twayne Publishers, 1965.

Joselyn, Sister M., O.S.B. " 'The Grave' as Lyrical Short Story." *Studies in Short Fiction*, 1 (1964): 216–21.

Liberman, M. M. *Katherine Anne Porter's Fiction*. Detroit: Wayne State University Press, 1971.

Lopez, Enrique Hank. *Conversations with Katherine Anne Porter: Refugee From Indian Creek*. Boston: Little, Brown and Co., 1981.

Marsden, M. M. "Love as a Threat in Katherine Anne Porter's Fiction." *Twentieth Century Literature* 13 (1967): 29–38.

Mooney, Harry John, Jr. *The Fiction and Criticism of Katherine Anne Porter*. Pittsburgh: University of Pittsburgh Press, 1957.

Nance, William L., S.M. *Katherine Anne Porter and the Art of Rejection*. Chapel Hill: University of North Carolina Press, 1964.

Prager, Leonard. "Getting and Spending: Porter's 'Theft'." *Perspective* 11 (1960): 230–34.

Reddin, Dorothy S. " 'Flowering Judas': Two Voices." *Studies in Short Fiction* (1969): 194–204.

Schwartz, Edward G. "The Fiction of Memory." *Southwest Review* 45 (1960): 204–15.

Solotaroff, Theodore. "*Ship of Fools* and the Critics." *Commentary* 34 (October 1962): 277–86.

Stein, William Bysshe. " 'Theft': Porter's Politics of Modern Love." *Perspective* 11 (Winter 1960): 223–28.

Waldrip, Louise and Bauer, Shirley Ann. *A Bibliography of the Works of Katherine Anne Porter* [and] *A Bibliography of the Criticism of the Works of Katherine Anne Porter*. Metuchen, N.J.: Scarecrow Press, 1969.

Walsh, Thomas F. "Miranda's Ghost in 'Old Mortality'." *College Literature* (1979): 56–63.

———. "Xochitl: Katherine Anne Porter's Changing Goddess." *American Literature* 52 (1980): 183–94.

Warren, Robert Penn, ed. *Katherine Anne Porter: A Collection of Critical Essays*. Englewood Cliffs, N.J.: Prentice-Hall, Inc., 1979.

West, Ray B., Jr. *Katherine Anne Porter*. Minneapolis: University of Minnesota Press, 1963.

Wolfe, Peter. "The Problems of Granny Weatherall." *CLA Journal* 2, vol. 11 (1967): 142–48.

Acknowledgments

"Irony with a Center" by Robert Penn Warren from *Selected Essays of Robert Penn Warren* by Robert Penn Warren, copyright © 1941 and 1969 by Robert Penn Warren. Reprinted by permission.

"*Ship of Fools*: Notes on Style" by Robert B. Heilman from *Katherine Anne Porter: A Critical Symposium* edited by George Core and Lodwick Hartley, copyright © 1969 by University of Georgia Press. Reprinted by permission.

"No Safe Harbor" by Howard Moss from *Writing Against Time: Critical Essays and Reviews* by Howard Moss, copyright © 1962 by Howard Moss. Reprinted by permission.

"The Eye of the Story" by Eudora Welty from *The Yale Review* (December 1965), copyright © 1965 by Eudora Welty. Reprinted by permission.

"Symbolism, the Short Story, and 'Flowering Judas' " by M. M. Liberman from *Katherine Anne Porter's Fiction* by M. M. Liberman, copyright © 1971 by Wayne State University Press. Reprinted by permission.

"Myth and Epiphany in Porter's 'The Grave' " by Constance Rooke and Bruce Wallis from *Studies in Short Fiction* 3, vol. 15 (Summer 1978), copyright © 1978 by Newberry College. Reprinted by permission.

"Katherine Anne Porter, Journalist" by Joan Givner from *Southwest Review* 4, vol. 64 (Autumn 1979), copyright © 1979 by Southern Methodist University. Reprinted by permission.

"The Dreams Self in 'Pale Horse, Pale Rider' " by Thomas F. Walsh from *Wascana Review* 2, vol. 14 (Fall 1979), copyright © 1980 by *Wascana Review*. Reprinted by permission.

"Pascal's Wager and Two Modern Losers" by Joann P. Cobb from *Philosophy and Literature* 2, vol. 3 (Fall 1979), copyright © 1979 by University of Michigan. Reprinted by permission.

" 'The Other Side of Silence': Katherine Anne Porter's 'He' as Tragedy" by Bruce

W. Jorgensen from *Modern Fiction Studies* 3, vol. 28 (Autumn 1982), copyright © 1982 by Purdue Research Foundation. Reprinted by permission.

"Narrative Irony and Hidden Motivations in Katherine Anne Porter's 'He' " by Debra A. Moddelmog from *Modern Fiction Studies* 3, vol. 28 (Autumn 1982), copyright © 1982 by Purdue Research Foundation. Reprinted by permission.

"Face to Face: 'Old Mortality' " by Jane Krause DeMouy from *Katherine Anne Porter's Women* by Jane Krause DeMouy, copyright © 1983 by University of Texas Press. Reprinted by permission.

Index